C. N. J. F. O.

Published by Gun For Hire LLC in the United States of America
Cover Art and Illustrations by Matt Dancsecs

The reason behind the way I am executing these illustrations with a touch of mechanical drawing is because this book is about creating a new civilian. One that can walk strong and is reworked to be more street smart. Re-engineered to become Crime Proof.

Gun For Hire LLC
1267 McBride Avenue
Woodland Park NJ, 07424
CrimeProofBook.com

DEDICATION

I would like to dedicate this book to the tens of thousands of students who have allowed me to educate them over the past thirty years. It is the novice seeking education and direction that keeps me going and gives me hope for our future.

I would also like to acknowledge all of my staff, friends, family, and my lady, Tracey Sarn, for putting up with all my "madness" for them to be safe and prepared. Many thanks also to Matt Dancsecs for the awesome cover and illustrations used throughout this book.

I also used an awesome cadre of peer reviewers for this book – John Petrolino, Tracey Sarn, Robert Prause, Tony Urena, Florence Colandro, Sandy Berardi, Kylie Rosado, Doug Herman, Thomas O'Beirne, Dylan Fitter, Kim Nehrings, and John Yiannou. I love and thank you all for the help, support, and encouragement.

For Winston (both of them).

Table of Contents

LEGAL DISCLAIMER

By reading and/or utilizing the information in this book, you acknowledge and agree that: (1) You alone are responsible for your reactions in any situation (collectively, "Conduct"); (2) this book is not a guarantee of personal safety in any situation, even if you properly follow its recommendations; (3) You will not hold the author, publisher, or copyright holder of this book (collectively, "Author") responsible for the consequences of your Conduct in any situation arising after reading this book (in whole or part); and (4) You will not bring or threaten to bring any claims against Author, and you irrevocably consent to the dismissal of any such claims. Do not utilize the information in this book if you do not agree to these terms.

PREFACE

So, you have decided to read a book on personal defense. Is it your first one or your 50th?

In the thirty years I have been teaching personal security, I have been told thousands of times, "You should write a book." I know you have all heard that cliché a thousand times. The truth is, in this business it is very hard to write a book on this subject because the rules keep changing. The criminals keep getting smarter and smarter; they are always finding new ways to rape us and pillage our possessions. I set out to write this book on personal defense and social responsibility to best cover a broad spectrum of options that I hope remain applicable for years to come. Most of the advice and tips in this book are perennial.

I hope that you never have to be on the receiving end of a violent encounter. I have survived three such encounters in the civilian world, and let me tell you, they trouble me to this day. But I am still here, so I must have done something right, or perhaps the day was mine. The fact that you are reading this book (or at least the introduction) indicates you are a person concerned for your and/or your family's security. This puts you in the category of "not prey." You see, predators look for prey and, unless they are really desperate, they will not pick someone that looks like they are alert or will fight back.

These traits put you in a distinct class. I call it the "don't mess with me" class. Reading material like this is a giant step in the right direction of protecting your most valuable assets, you and your family.

Welcome, enjoy, and be safe!

CHAPTER
01

Are You Prepared?

So, you're reading my book. What is unfortunate is that most people who will read my book don't need it, because they're actively seeking out better ways to secure themselves and their family. This mentality normally makes you the alpha, the one who wants to make sure your family is safe. The people who need to read this book are the ones who need to be force fed the knowledge.

There always seems to be one person who takes the responsibility of the family's safety and well-being. That person is normally the alpha male. Now, of course, with today's society, we have households that are run by the alpha woman, two women, or two men, and in the soft society we have managed to cultivate, sometimes we're lacking an alpha altogether. It is our job, me the writer and you the reader, to figure out how we can increase the security and safety of our loved ones by getting it through their heads that evil does exist, and yes, it can happen to them. Too many people let their guard down and think it could never happen to them. How wrong are they?

Violent crime statistics continue to grow in our country due to our catch-and-release, revolving-door criminal justice system. The predators walk amongst us– on the street, in the mall shopping with our children, on our playgrounds, and even right next door to us. There is no lack of proof in our news cycles indicating this.

We have all heard of the color code system for our national security. We can use the same color code system for our home planning, home defense, and mentality overall, including outside the home. The original color code system was invented by Colonel Jeff Cooper, who is arguably the master of modern pistol craft.

Cooper said that the lowest condition we have is Condition White. I like to refer to Condition White as "total unawareness of endangerment." A perfect example of Condition White would be: you're in your house, all the doors are locked, the alarm system is on, and you and your loved ones are watching a movie in the living room. That's a time for your body to wind down in Condition White, where you can relax and give your brain a little break.

Unfortunately, in our society, you have people that walk the streets in Condition White. Predators love prey in Condition White. You'll see people walking in the mall, you'll see tourists traveling in the trendy areas, basically with the head-in-the-ass disease in full bloom, not looking around, not aware of their surroundings, mulling along, typing on their phone, talking into their phone, looking down towards the ground. This is the predator's buffet.

The next level of awareness would be Condition Yellow. Let's go back to sitting in your living room with the doors locked and the alarm on with your family, and you hear a noise outside. It's not an organic noise; it's a noise you've maybe never heard before. Your ears perk up a little bit. Maybe the dog's head lifts up from the rug. That would put you in Condition Yellow. Another example of Condition Yellow would be when you're walking down the street on your commute or going out for a nice walk in the evening, or shopping in a mall. Condition Yellow would be walking with your shoulders back, your chest out, a nice erect position, walking with purpose. You'd be scanning left to right, making eye contact, still enjoying whatever you're doing with your family, but just keeping aware of all of your surroundings. You're not being aggressive or issuing menacing looks, but you're aware.

Most people who go through life in Condition Yellow tend to have an aversion to going to venues with large amounts of people, like sports games, enclosed malls, or concerts. I am one of those. You cannot stay in Condition Yellow for long periods of time without starting to feel some psychological stress and some psychological fatigue. We all need to go into Condition White once in a while to recharge our batteries. The problem is trying to get our liabilities, our non-alphas, to wake up and be aware of their surroundings and stay in Condition Yellow. Your non-alpha liabilities can be children, the elderly, aloof friends, or your significant other.

Next is Condition Orange. Following Cooper's principles, Condition Orange is when you're in that living room again with your family, and you repetitiously hear that non-organic noise, and the dog perks up and starts growling, and you become very aware that something is wrong outside. This would put us into Condition Orange.

The dog perks up, you hear the noise repetitiously. It might be the sound of breaking glass or something being pried open, and you know it's not normal. In turn, you would snap into Condition Orange. This is when it's time to get prepared, and you better have a plan. How many times have we been in Condition Orange? How many times have we heard the doorbell ring at three in the morning, or a picture falls off of the wall in the middle of the night?

When you wake up, that's Condition Orange. Condition Orange means something is coming, and you better be ready for it. The problem is, most people at that point are on the fly, devising their self-defense plan from that point on, when your plan should have been developed already. A plan is only good for the first five seconds, so it's always going to be a dynamic thing that is going to change. But you need to be mentally ready, because implementing a part of a plan is better than no plan at all.

Another example of Condition Orange would be walking down a street on the way home from work and realizing that someone is following you. After making a series of turns, you notice that they're still following you. That would be the opportunity for you to wake up and get into Condition Orange and be prepared, whether it's calling 911 from your cell phone or stepping into a store and waiting for help to arrive. These are just a few examples of the levels that we need to be in tune with.

The last level would be Condition Red. Condition Red can be compared to any shit-has-hit-the-fan moment. Condition Red is a situation of action—you must act. Condition Red kicks in when the bad guy puts the knife to your throat and asks you for your money, or when your purse is ripped from your arm. Maybe your back door is smashed open and someone is heading towards you with intent to do harm to you and your family.

It is at that point when the battle is on that there are many psychological facets you have to deal with. When someone is confronted with a violent encounter or Condition Red, their "lizard brain" will kick in. The "lizard brain" is slang for the amygdala, the portion of the brain responsible for one's fight or flight reflexes.

You may also freeze in a situation like this, and that is not always bad, as long as you use that time to plan the next move you will take. At Gun For Hire, we promote the concept of OODA loop. The OODA loop was developed by John Boyd, a Colonel with the US Air Force. OODA stands for: observe, orient, decide, and act. He applied this concept to the combat operations process, often at the operational level during military campaigns. OODA is now often applied to understanding a learning process. This process shows the way agility can overcome raw power in dealing with opponents. According to Boyd, decision-making follows these steps. Someone that is able to run through these steps quickly can "get inside" the thought process of an adversary. The ability to execute OODA will give you an advantage. So you see, even if you are frozen, you can tactfully use that time to gain an advantage over your attacker.

The amygdala essentially sounds the alarm in your brain. A number of things happen once the alarm is sounded. The most prominent thing that occurs is the release of adrenaline (epinephrine), which is produced by the adrenal glands. We call this phenomenon an adrenaline dump. This is responsible for giving us the boost we need to deal with such encounters. The physical changes that occur during an adrenaline dump all revolve around putting energy and resources to work for your immediate needs.

One such change would be something called "Tunnel Vision." Your focus in on the bad guy, and you can't see around you. Your peripheral vision is shut out, and only the portion of the eye that is responsible for acute focus is actually working. Your pupils will dilate. You have to physically scan by turning your head in order to see what might be happening in the area around a threat.

Another phenomenon would be "Time Dilation," where the entire encounter seems to happen frame-by-frame, in slow motion. If anyone reading this has ever been in a car accident before, you'll know what I'm talking about.

An additional aspect of your "lizard brain" kicking in would be "Auditory Exclusion." With Auditory Exclusion, you can't hear anything around you, or the sounds are muted. Someone could be yelling and calling you to run in a certain direction or come to them for aid, and you might not be able to hear them.

Something else that will occur during an adrenaline dump is blood vessel constriction. The blood vessels in your appendages will constrict (vasoconstriction), allowing blood flow to be concentrated to your more important organs. When this happens, your fine motor skills will be diminished, and you'll be relying on gross motor skills. It would be difficult to grasp and manipulate items with your hands. When this is happening, your heart rate, blood pressure, and breathing rate (respiration) will increase.

The body shuts down what is not necessary when it's in the Condition Red mode, because it's all about basic survival skills. I'll reiterate, this is why you need a rehearsed plan, conditioning yourself to hopefully act without further panic. Are you prepared?

You're on your way to becoming prepared. But how do you get this message across to your family and friends? Especially your wife, husband, children, etc. This is not an easy task. To be able to impart these concepts to your spouse and children without scaring them to death, to a point where they might never want to leave the house, is a very thin line that we have to make sure we do not cross. Children are the hardest to instill any type of defensive training in because, by nature, children have good hearts and do not see evil in things. Women are the second hardest because they always feel, when presented with statistics, that it could never happen to them. They'll tell us we're crazy and it happens to other people, these things you read in the newspaper, but it can never happen to them. They may call you paranoid.

How many women, or people in general, do we observe when we're walking through a mall or food store parking lot that are totally unaware of their surroundings? They'd be talking or texting on a cell phone, or digging in their purse or pockets for their keys as they approach their car. These people are usually leaving a child in a shopping carriage while they turn their back, 180 degrees, to put bags in the car. How many times have we all seen that? It's a very hard topic to broach with our loved ones without them getting defensive and calling you "crazy." But the fact is, just a few small lessons in defensive training and awareness can go a very long way in preventing a predator from picking you or your loved ones as prey. Benjamin Franklin was quoted as saying "An ounce of prevention is worth a pound of cure." It's better to get ahead of a problem versus having to deal with one.

With children, we teach them early on, "don't talk to strangers." The game and rules have changed. Now, we need to teach our children to be aware of strangers and not just not talk to them, but be aware of them and keep away from them. We need to teach our children that there are evil and bad people out there. It's our responsibility and their responsibility to help keep them safe. This is not an easy task. Every child is different; every child matures differently. The last thing you want to do is give your child nightmares. The worst thing you could do is not train them at all and put them at risk for the rest of their life. So, it is every parent's responsibility to have an understanding of their child's maturity level and decide how much information they can give them. As your children mature, you can make them more and more aware of the evils that exist in our society.

I have usually found over the past 30 years of training that, when it comes to training a spouse or immediate family member, it is best to seek professional help. I don't mean that as a psychiatrist's help. I mean that it's like trying to teach your spouse how to drive a stick shift, and the old adage is that you'll end up divorced. I've just seen too many times where the husband will be sincere in trying to teach a skill to his spouse and the wife will not take it seriously, or vice versa. The scenario ends up in an argument between the two. Couples bring their relationship baggage with them wherever they go. For example, if one partner in a relationship does not think their counterpart folds laundry the "right" way, or does the dishes the "right" way, what makes anyone think that those biases won't make their way into a teaching session at a shooting range, or into any other moment of instruction? And yet the spouse or family member will learn from the "professional" and do whatever the professional recommends. The same applies to children.

In the following chapters, I will be giving you some great personal defense and awareness strategies for you and your family. What you can do is drop these little pearls of wisdom every day as you encounter and observe different situations, or point out people letting their guard down that are not related or associated to you. An example would be: as you're driving through the mall parking lot, say to your wife, "Hon, look how that woman is putting the bags in the car but she's not keeping an eye on her child in the cart!" Or, saying to your eleven-year-old daughter, "Look at that girl, how she's texting with her head down and she's totally unaware of her surroundings, how someone can just come up from behind her, grab her, and she would never know what happened!" These are ways that we can indirectly instill these personal defense strategies into our loved ones without personally directing it towards them. I have found that, if deployed properly, you will experience your loved ones repeating to you what you told them a week or two earlier. This is a win/win situation for everyone. Presentation is the key, and direct presentation is not always the best way to get a point across.

How do we, as responsible adults, instill safety training without creating nightmares or phobias in our children that make them afraid to leave the house? This is a very hard question to address. But you have to understand that there are subtle, indirect ways to bring personal defense strategies to light without directly scaring and scarring our loved ones. The vast majority of television series today are police shows, or at least have some degree of violence in them. Many parents try to shield their children from such shows, but the violence is everywhere, from older cartoons to modern video games.

A perfect example: In my house, twice a year when we change the clocks, I change the batteries in the smoke and carbon monoxide detectors, check the levels of the fire extinguishers, and swap out my magazines on my home defense firearms. If I have any digital lock boxes or safes, I'd change the batteries in those too. In the household, I'd have a fire drill, and then we'd have an "emergency drill." I do not call it a "home invasion drill" or a "boogie man is coming through the basement drill." I call it an emergency drill. We'd review what to do in case there is an emergency. This routine is gone through every six months, and it has worked very well so far. Keep things toned down slightly, without losing the importance of the message. The key element is building a sound foundation so other skills and concepts can be further built upon it.

In the next chapter, we're going to take the defensive mindset further, and we're going to talk about some strategies that we can use to make sure our family hones their skills, and then I'm going to give some tips on how we can test them.

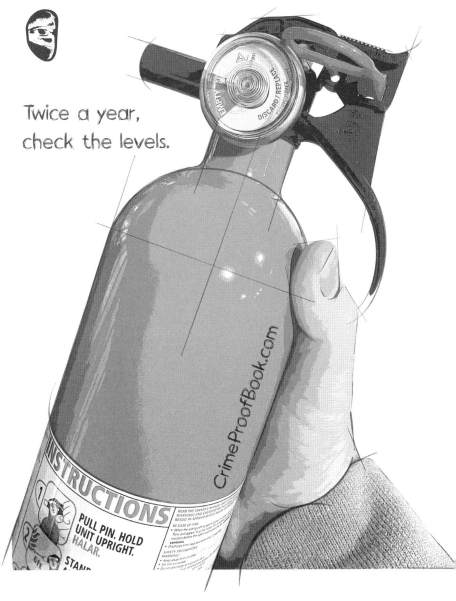

Twice a year, check the levels.

CrimeProofBook.com

CHAPTER
02
Defining the Defensive Mindset

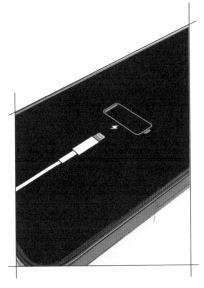

In this chapter, I want to try to define the Defensive Mindset. A Defensive Mindset is someone's head who's wired to always be in Condition Yellow unless they're locked in the house with the alarm on, in the confines of their own home or domicile, with all of their family safe and sound with them. Now, many of you reading this book, you probably already have a Defensive Mindset. How many of you that are reading this book right now, when you go to a restaurant, want to sit with your back to the wall so that you can watch the entrance? THAT makes YOU a person with the Defensive Mindset. And how many of your family members give you crap because they can't understand why you want to have that defensive seating position? I follow the hostess to pick the tactical seat, another Condition Yellow trick I employ whenever I eat out. A few weeks ago, I went to dinner with Tracey and two other couples, one I knew and one I met for the first time. The ploy is, I volunteer to check with the hostess to see if our table is ready. When it is, I announce it and follow the hostess closely, so I get to choose the best tactical seat at the table! Defensive Mindset people also tend to be the ones who want to drive the car when traveling because they want to be in control.

I fall into this category. I have a Defensive Mindset, and it has been my calling in life to teach other people to be alert and aware, and to have a Defensive Mindset. It is not always easy. People slip out of it all the time. People who normally have a Defensive Mindset NEVER slip out of it completely. It NEVER goes away. Perfect example: It's three a.m. My dog, Winston, starts barking. My ex-wife says, "Shut up!" to the dog. I look at her and say, "The dog is barking at three a.m. for a reason." I get up, I go look, and there's a car double-parked in front of my house, running with the interior light on. Three a.m., and a gentleman is text messaging. When he's done, he shuts the interior light off and he pulls away. But my dog sensed that because dogs, by nature, are Defensive Mindset machines. As a human, I understand that the dog is barking for a reason, and it's my job to help him with his job to go and look and see why. My ex, on the other hand, who does not have a natural Defensive Mindset, feels it's proper to yell at the dog for doing his job. That is the difference. This is the lifelong battle that people with Defensive Mindsets will have to deal with compared to people who do not have Defensive Mindsets.

What's the difference between the two? Take someone who doesn't have a Defensive Mindset, let them be a victim of a mugging or a robbery, and watch what happens to them after that. Watch how their body language is different, how they stand near the ticket counter on a subway platform, how they stand with their back to a telephone or a light pole at a bus stop on the corner. You'll notice all these things. Those of us with Defensive Mindsets seek out and search out ways to use the environment and the world to our advantage to help shore up our defenses. People without a Defensive Mindset just amble along carelessly day to day to day until a predator spots them and decides to make them prey.

Keeping your Defensive Mindset sharp requires much work. Of course, if you have young children that you bring to a mall or an outdoor park, you're constantly watching them. I know many reading this book who are of that mindset. How many times have you been to the park and you see a parent who's talking on a cell phone and their kids are playing unattended? The parent is not even watching them! THIS is someone who doesn't have a Defensive Mindset. If there is any time to adopt the "Papa Bear" or "Momma Bear" mentality, it is when you're in public with your children!

We need to cultivate, we need to hone, and we need to sharpen our Defensive Mindset every day. We should constantly be reading people, reading the room, and sitting in a spot that's closest to the fire exit. We should walk towards oncoming traffic when we're walking, but should we walk right against the curb, or should we walk about three feet from the curb? Too many people take this for granted. When I'm driving down the street and I see someone walk right out into the street and open the driver's side door of their car without even looking at me oncoming, I know that they're in Condition White. These are the people that you read about, that girl who was text messaging or adjusting her radio when driving. These are the people that run other people over, and we wonder how that happens. We have all seen people in crosswalks ignoring traffic, as they feel they have the right of way, thereby pitting a 150-pound pedestrian against a 3,000-pound automobile. Most…MOST of our encounters where we're subjected to being hurt or a victim are self-induced. This is not about victim shaming, in no way. This is about an individual's level of awareness.

Many negative encounters are preventable. It does not require a lot of your time. It does not require additional money. All that it requires is to be constantly vigilant and constantly aware of our surroundings.

Can we not identify a seasoned city dweller from a tourist as they're walking down the street? I'm not just talking about the way they're dressed. I'm talking about the way they act. Someone who is a commuter in a large city, especially if there happens to be a high crime rate, will walk with a determined pace to them, making eye contact; looking and scanning left to right. A tourist, on the other hand, is looking around in wonder, totally not aware of their surroundings. That is because your city commuter has gone to great lengths, gained survival skills, and gone through much conditioning to get that Defensive Mindset. An edge, if you will. People with Defensive Mindsets tend to not drink more than one or two drinks socially because they also do not like to lose control of their surroundings or their situation.

A key concept to understand concerning a Defensive Mindset is something called "normalcy bias." This is someone's predisposition to disbelieve or be dismissive of potential threats or things that might be out of order. This concept can be summed up by the "It won't happen to me" mentality that people have. This can include people seeing something that is not quite right, but trying to rationalize it to themselves, or maybe others, for assurance. Normalcy bias leaves people unprepared for adverse situations. Someone who questions why you prepare for things, or may even call you paranoid for adhering to some of the precepts in this book, suffers from a form of normalcy bias. Want to get caught with your pants down? Adopt normalcy bias and remain blissfully ignorant of the potential threats to you and your family.

Now that I am making you aware of it, you will notice this. How many times have you come home, and your porch light is not working or your garage light is not working? I, as someone with a Defensive Mindset, question why it's not working. Someone who does not have a Defensive Mindset goes, "Oh, the bulb probably burned out." I realize that the bulb probably burned out, but I don't trust that. Until I verify that the bulb burned out on its own, it's my job to make sure nothing is going on. That is a clear difference between someone with a Defensive Mindset and someone without a Defensive Mindset. Don't explain away anomalies; figure out what is going on first, and once your safety and security is secured, then come to a conclusion. But don't just jump to a conclusion of regularity.

It is not easy being the one with a Defensive Mindset. It is not easy at all. We're constantly vigilant, we're constantly aware of our surroundings. We try to instill this in our loved ones when they leave the house. When we say "be careful" to our loved ones, we really mean it, and we know that, many times, our loved ones are walking around malls and public places in Condition White. It is our job to train, re-train, and test our friends and family so that they can walk through life in Condition Yellow just like us.

Defensive Mindset people are constantly charging their cell phones.

A great example is when we're at an amusement park, and after warning the children repeatedly, "Do not separate from us," I did a test while walking over a footbridge where I let my youngest nephew walk ahead of us, and we all hid behind a piling on the bridge. Well, my nephew walked about 25 or 30 feet, stopped, looked 360 degrees, and realized we were all nowhere to be found. A look of terror shot through his face, and he started screaming for his mother. It was at that point I stepped out from behind the support on the bridge. He saw me and came running towards me. Then I grabbed him, and I explained to him how important it is to stay nearby, how easy it is to be separated from us, and what the consequences could be. I noticed that, for the rest of the day, he stood very close to us when we walked through the park from that point on.

Another real and simple example of Defensive Mindset is, the person with the Defensive Mindset will tend to only let their car get to about a half-tank of gasoline before they fill up again. Someone who doesn't have a Defensive Mindset will let the car run all the way to "E" before they stop and refill. Why does this seem to not fit and yet fits together? Because, if there was a catastrophe or an emergency and you had to high-tail it home or high-tail it out of town, how far are you going to get with half a gallon of gas in your tank? If any loved ones in your house run the needle to "E" on their gas tank, you need to start working on them to get a Defensive Mindset.

Another scenario of someone with a Defensive Mindset and someone without a Defensive Mindset is, Defensive Mindset people are ALWAYS charging their cell phones. They're always on a dock, they're always attached to a charging cable, whether they're in the car, the office, or the house. Someone who does not have a Defensive Mindset will let their phone run down to one bar or 20% before their brain turns on and says, "Maybe I should charge this." Everyone reading this, can you pick out the family members and those that you work with who are of a Defensive Mindset or NOT of the Defensive Mindset? You will notice that on a lot of people. When my phone gets below 50%, I start to panic. I also keep a phone charger in all of my vehicles.

The list of what separates those who employ this mindset and those that do not can go on in perpetuity. Other little examples revolve around questions such as: "Do you have an alarm system?" and "Do you have a motion-activated doorbell cam?" When you get an alarm signal, do you always assume it's a "false" alarm, because they are frequent? If that is the case, you need to reevaluate the quality of your system and/or reconfigure it. With the doorbell cam, do you ignore the notifications you get because the majority of them are cars big enough to trigger it?

These are questions and concepts that you need to think about and evaluate. Shutting out our own normalcy biases to hone our Defensive Mindset involves thought and practice. Don't be dismissive to alerts you get. Don't become complacent. Your alarm should be zoned to different rooms, doors, and windows, and should be connected to your cell phone. You may get a burglar alarm, but if it's not an exterior door or a window, and you are home or not home, it could be a mouse or a picture falling off the wall. That may save a lot of worry and the need for a police response. It is important to have your settings zeroed in and follow up on any malfunctions.

Here is a great example of a Defensive Mindset in the era of cell phones. How many phone numbers do you have memorized in case there's an emergency and you don't have your phone? Test some of your friends and family members as well. If there is an emergency and you were separated from your cell phone, who could you call? I honestly only know my number and the Gun For Hire Range's number. You see, I also need to refocus sometimes as well.

Little "tells" like these are what differentiate people of a Defensive Mindset and people that don't have a Defensive Mindset. It's our job to train and cultivate the loved ones around us that do not have the Defensive Mindset. Again, this is not an easy task, and it doesn't always have its rewards, believe me. No good deed goes unpunished. I can tell you countless times where I've tried to "brainwash" loved ones on what they're doing wrong by subjecting themselves to predators and becoming prey, only to have them push back and argue with me and tell me I'm crazy, saying I don't know what I'm talking about, I overreact, and I worry too much. Yes, I am guilty of all of the above. But also, yes, I have made it into my sixties, I've survived encounters, and I'm still here today to talk about it.

CHAPTER
03
Defensive Positions

We are going to discuss some important information in this chapter in the event that an intruder comes into your home or workplace. These ideas should also be applied outside of the home in areas like parking garages, shopping malls, etc. This might be difficult to think about, but it's very important, so pay close attention.

There are two things to think about when you are thinking about defense—cover and concealment. Cover is something that will protect you from a bullet. Concealment is a place that you can hide so an intruder may not see you. Do a mental survey of your home in your mind and think about what is cover and what is concealment. Do the same for your workplace. Draw up some hypotheticals for when you're out and about, living your life.

For example, in your home: hiding behind a couch or a refrigerator would be concealment. Cover would be hiding behind the engine block of your car or a cement wall in your basement. An exterior wall would be cover. Solid doors could be cover in some instances, but not all. This depends on the door as well as the caliber of the firearm being used.

There's not a lot of cover in an average house, so you have to focus on the element of surprise. You have to use that concealment to your advantage. As mentioned earlier, concealment options could include a couch or refrigerator. Perhaps long flowing curtains. A closet. Being around the corner of a wall. You get the idea. Anything that would mask you from being seen.

If someone was trying to break into your house, and you were home and heard them, the best idea would be to move to the room you've made up for this situation. We call this a safe room, or an Alamo room, where you would make your last stand. If you use a bedroom or any other room, there needs to be a deadbolt lock on the inside of the door. A key thing to remember is to try to keep all of your loved ones behind you wherever you are, because it's the best defensive position. Try to get past the children's bedrooms and maintain high ground at the top of stairs. But don't stand at the top of stairs; instead, get in a prone or kneeling position. If someone turns a corner and looks upstairs, you would be a short target. When the intruder turns a corner, his or her eyes would look up, not down. You will have a few seconds of advantage as they register what they are seeing. Then you announce to the intruder: "Get out of the house. Do not come upstairs. I called the police. I have a gun, and I will use it."

If you and your loved ones are all in the safe room you've chosen, should you go look for the intruder? If everyone you care about is with you, don't go look. Call 911, give your address, describe the situation, and stay on the line until the police come. Of course, if you have loved ones in a downstairs bedroom, you have to go look. We will discuss safe rooms and options later in this book.

Once you all get into your safe room, if it's a bedroom, get on the far side of bed and kneel with your elbows on the mattress with your gun, if you have one, trained on the point of entry. We call this a fatal funnel, where you are trying to force them to follow a cone-shaped path where they will be most vulnerable to you. Keeping your elbows on the mattress will alleviate the physical stress of holding your firearm. You don't know how long you'll be hunkered down. To note, an exercise

Fatal funnel, where you are trying to force them to follow a cone-shaped path where they will be most vulnerable to you.

you can do would be to hold up a two-pound weight, with your arms stretched out in front of you. Visualize you are holding a pistol that is keeping an intruder held at gunpoint. How long can you do it? While you're getting situated, have your kids lay down on floor on the far side of bed. It will offer excellent concealment for them. Being low and close to the ground will make them "smaller" as well. You should have your cell phone on the bed next to you, talking to the police. You want a record on 911 of you telling the intruder that you have called the police and that you have a gun and will use it. This recording is admissible in court, and you'll want everyone to hear you loudly warning the intruder and stating what your actions will be. Your lawyer will thank me.

Your workplace cover and concealment options are going to depend on what kind of occupation you have. If you're an office worker in a cubicle or open space, your options for cover are going to be limited. You may have plenty of concealment options, such as desks and dividers. If you work in a more industrial setting, you may have both good cover and concealment, depending on your industry. Work around heavy machinery? Heavy machinery may stop bullets without issue. How about a construction site? Big steel I-beams and concrete structures could afford good cover.

Being outside of the home, in an unfamiliar setting, is a wild card. If you're tooling around a big shopping mall, hiding behind one of those big plants in the concrete planters may do you no good. A clothing rack in a department store may be large enough to give you great concealment. Parking garages can offer cover in the way of the concrete support beams. Everything is going to be situationally dependent, especially outside the home, and the decision to take cover/concealment over fleeing is one you'll have to make in split seconds.

While you add to your gambit of options, further fortifying your Defensive Mindset, remember cover and concealment. Concealment is hiding (i.e. light materials, cloth, fibers, wood, etc.), and cover is protection (i.e., heavy materials, steel, concrete, and bulletproof glass).

CHAPTER
04
Home Protection

There is no black and white when it comes to protecting your home. Every home is different. Every layout is unique. So, as the dwellers in our home, we have to look at it and decide how we can harden the defenses and set up a good home defense plan. Creating safe rooms on different floors and in different areas of the home is very important and, believe it or not, it's inexpensive. It's not expensive to set your house up to protect you and your family better. It just requires a vigilance to use the devices that you have at your disposal. How many times have we come home, and the sliding glass door is unlocked on our house? Sliding doors are so easily defeated. All the sliding doors in my house have a "Charlie bar" installed so the only way to gain entry is to break the window. How many times have we come home, and the inside door is open

Installed charlie bar

between the garage and our dwelling? How many times have we come home, and there's a ground floor window open and nobody's home in the house? How many of you reading this have alarm systems and haven't turned them on, or haven't turned them on in so long, you don't even remember what the code is? These are things that I see every day in my business.

Let's talk about the big picture here. The first thing we should talk about is, every house, at minimum, should have one safe room. Now, the safe room doesn't need to be like the one in the Jody Foster movie where you have steel walls and oxygen piped in. When you have a safe room, preferably it's a room that has an egress window, like a bedroom or a bathroom, and all you need to do is have a solid-core door with a reinforced door frame and a deadbolt lock. This is a room that you could readily or easily escape to, lock the door, and buy you and your family some valuable time until help arrives. That time can also be used to get your defensive firearm out, or whatever other tool you might use to protect yourself and your family. My bedroom has a door that swings out. I learned this trick because drug dealing houses and methamphetamine labs always have the exterior doors swing out because it is much harder to kick or shoulder a door in that's resting against its frame, as opposed to a door that's only resting against the lock. It might be a little uncomfortable to have a layout like this in some houses and ergonomically it might not work out, but it is by far the best layout to have. If a door swings out, the two or three sets of hinges are exposed. An intruder with a screwdriver or a knife can pry the hinge out and pull open the door. The door should have hinges with non-removable pins. They are commercially available.

When I remodeled my home, I had my contractor replace every door in the house for the bathrooms and the bedrooms with solid-core doors. The price difference was nominal compared to hollow-core doors. Then all of my bathrooms and bedrooms have a blind deadbolt lock mounted one-third of the way down from the top of the door frame. A blind deadbolt means there's no keyhole in the front of the door; it's smooth, just the wood is exposed. But on the inside of the door is the thumb-tab or lever that's used to lock the door. In my house, in any room you can run in and you can flip over that deadbolt, and you've just created a safe room that can buy you valuable seconds or minutes. I understand that having a blind deadbolt like this might not be the right tactic for those that have children who may want to lock mom and dad out, but you need to be the deciding factor, weighing your options on something like this.

One of the most important things to have in your safe room is a cell phone. Most people carry their cell phones on them today all the time. Another trick is, old cell phones, even if they're not connected to service anymore, can dial 911. It's not a bad idea to take a handful of your old cell phones and put one in each room connected to a charger, behind a bureau or on top of a nightstand, and have them sitting there should you ever need them to dial 911 in an emergency.

The plans that you make when you hold an emergency planning meeting or drill with your family or with yourself is, you have to think about your environment, and you're about to read the words "visualization" and "mindset" many times. Most people think that when a home invasion or a home break-in occurs, it's when you're in the bedroom, when the fact of the matter is, many home invasions or break-ins occur in the evening or during the day when the family is home, doing whatever they normally do in the kitchen, living room, dining room, or family room. Your job is to use visualization to determine, if we were sitting in the living room and someone broke in, which direction would we go? What plan would we implement? If we were in the bedroom, what would we do? If we were in the basement, what would we do? These are questions that need to be asked and addressed. Will the plan be fully implemented should an emergency occur? Probably not, but better than to waste valuable seconds in time debating "Should I run left, or should I run right?"

because just maybe your instincts and training will kick in and you won't question or doubt yourself, you'll run in the correct direction, and you'll be able to secure yourself and your family until help arrives. Just remember, every house is unique. Every house will require different levels of training. Every house will require a different level of vigilance. We never ever rise to the occasion, but rather we fall to the level of our own training.

Some of the items that you should consider having in your safe room(s) would be flashlights. Many manufacturers make flashlights that plug right into an outlet in the room, which keeps them charged all the time and, should there be a power failure, there's a little night light that goes on. I find those very valuable. I have one in every room in the house. Again, I'm referred to as the "family crazy," but the first time we had a power failure in the house and my ex was in the basement washing clothes, it was total darkness. The night light lit on the spare flashlight that was plugged in between the washer and the dryer, and she was able to pull it out of the plug, turn it on, and walk upstairs. It was at that point she told me that the flashlights were, in fact, a good idea. It seems that they do work. Flashlights are good for multiple reasons. The flashlights not only fulfill their intended purpose, to see in the darkness, but they are also good for shining out the window to give police or first responders your

Blackout flashlights are key.

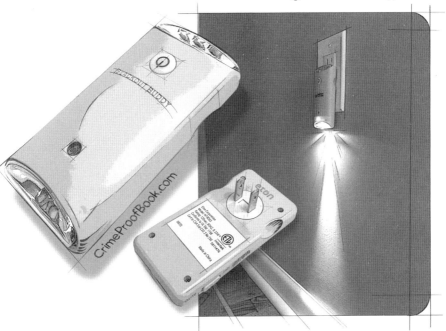

location. Flashlights are good for temporarily blinding any type of attacker or aggressor as well. Once I was traveling in Boston, and my lady and I were taking a stroll after dinner; it was dark, and there were only a few people on the streets. We were approached by a man who asked to see my watch. I said no and he said, "I am going to take it." At that point I pulled my flashlight out of my left pocket and pushed the tail piece in and hit him in the face with 200 lumens of light! Well, you would have thought I threw acid in his face! He raised his hands and went flying back like I blinded him as we proceeded to swiftly walk

200 lumens of light in the face.

CrimeProofBook.com

away. Threat over. I like a small tail button activated light with a strike bezel for everyday carry.

Another item you should have in your safe room, and this I got from the NRA "Refuse to be a Victim" Program (which is registered to the NRA), are light sticks, the crack-and-shake, glow-in-the-dark light sticks that people use at parties and concerts. We teach in our school, from the NRA, to take a spare front door key, attach it to a light stick, and keep it in a nightstand in a safe room. If you're locked in your safe room and you feel that the perpetrators might still be in the house when the police arrive, rather than opening your door and walking through the house to let the police in, you can crack the light stick, shake it, and throw it out the window. The police can use it to let themselves in. I find this to be a very invaluable tool to have in a safe room.

You should have an axe and Kevlar gloves to break out a window if necessary, and a rope ladder with sill hooks to escape. Also, you should determine which window has

Front door key + light stick.

CrimeProofBook.com

the least amount of distance to the ground and provides the safest fall.

Of course, being a "gun guy," a defensive firearm would be a great asset to have in your safe room as well. We're going to cover this in another chapter, because it merits its own chapter due to the extensive information we have to cover. Naturally, a firearm is not for everyone, and you may be reading this and thinking you don't want a firearm. That's fine. But as long as you're in a Defensive Mindset and you walk around in a heightened state of awareness with purpose, it kind of minimizes your chances of ever having to use a defensive firearm. I also have a few edged weapons and pepper sprays in my safe room as well.

One thing I'm asked all the time is, "If I'm in the house and I lock myself or myself and my loved ones in the safe room or bedroom, and I heard noises, then they seem to have subsided, should I go look?" This is something I've heard numerous times. If you and your loved ones are all huddled up in a safe area, my advice to you is NEVER go look. You are not a trained police officer. You are not a trained special weapons and tactics officer. Clearing a room is not an easy job to do. Room-to-room searches to find a possibly armed intruder is not for the average citizen. Wait for the police to arrive and let them look.

A scenario that's a little different: If one of my children was sleeping on the first floor, and my wife and

I were with the younger children in the second floor safe room, it would be my obligation to take my firearm, flashlight, or whatever weapon I have at my disposal to go and secure my child downstairs. I'd be willing to take a risk at that point. But if we're all secure in a bedroom or a safe room, there really is no reason to go looking around, because any material property can be replaced. It's your loved ones that cannot be replaced.

Additional tips on home protection

Back in the day when I was a child, everyone was told if someone knocked on the door, don't answer. Well, the rules of engagement have changed today because what happens is, we have these smash-and-grab robbers out there that will knock on the front door and, if there's no answer, they'll take a crowbar out and smash the door in. They'll run into your house, run right to the master bedroom, grab any electronics or any jewelry they can grab, and run back out. An important note about that master bedroom: most smash-and-grab criminals will hit all the top drawers of dressers and bureaus. Why? Because that is where many people store their "important" stuff. Don't keep cash, passports, social security cards, firearms, etc. in the top drawers of your dressers, no matter how many pairs of socks or underwear you have on top of them. Your

Aerosmith T-Shirt from back in the day is not going to keep your belongings safe! If you have kids, you can stash valuables in their rooms. It is the last place thieves go to look. There are also many options for hiding or stashing valuables with little or no cost. In the old days, organized crime kept their money in the freezer wrapped in foil wrap!

If you have an alarm system and the main point of entry is your front door, there's a good chance that you'll have a 45-second delay on that alarm. After the 45-second delay, the alarm company receives the signal. What's going to happen is, the alarm company will call your house to see if it was a false alarm or not. In some cases, if a secondary and tertiary number is listed, they will call those numbers too. If no one answers, or someone does from an alternate number and they indicate no one is supposed to be home, they're going to dispatch the police. The average police response time in the United States currently is 11 minutes. We've just given a burglar a nice six- or seven-minute window to come in and ransack your house, with plenty of time as all the numbers are called and police dispatched.

If our children or teenage children are standing behind that door and they don't respond, they're going to be standing there when the bad guy breaks into the house. So, you see, the rules have changed today. What we need our children and other adults in the house to know is that they should answer through the door, "Hello, who is it?" A great ruse would be to say, "My dad is sleeping right now, and he doesn't like if I wake him." The child or other family member should have their phone in their hand (most young kids live with their phones in their hands today).

If the person doesn't leave or it looks fishy, they should immediately dial 911. When the 911 call center answers, a lot of times the dispatcher will ask, "State the emergency." This is incorrect. The proper thing to do is to teach yourself and your family to say your address two times clearly and concisely and then state the emergency. The 911 call system in our country, which is second to none, is really not equipped to handle cellular phone calls. What if you're calling from a cell phone that's owned by your job and the address is your work address? If you get knocked off the phone, the police are going to dispatch to your work rather than your home. Therefore, it's very important to teach everyone to say their address two times, clear and concise, state the emergency, and then stay on the line. It will do you no good if your family member or young child calls you up to say there's a stranger on the front porch. All you're doing is wasting valuable minutes and putting them at risk. Remember that privacy issues do not allow the phone company to reveal your information without a subpoena or an emergent order. Cell phones can be traced for location but not exact locations. Depending on cell tower locations, they can only give approximate location.

Another tactic criminals may use is for a delivery person to knock on the door and say they have a delivery and get you to open the door. If it's an unsolicited delivery, I say be very wary. In New Jersey, in 2008, a woman answered her front door for a flower delivery, and when she opened the door she was knocked to the ground and tied up. The white van backed into the driveway and two perpetrators ransacked the entire house. She was asked why she opened the door for a stranger. She stated it was her 35th wedding anniversary, and she figured the flowers were delivered from her husband. What had happened was, two weeks prior, they had paid painters to come in and paint the interior of the house, and she had a calendar on the side of the refrigerator. She had the day of the home invasion circled in red marker, and had written out "Our 35th Wedding Anniversary" as a reminder for her husband. Well, one of the bad guys took note of that and passed it on to friends, and low and behold, she was set up on the day of their wedding anniversary.

With modern social media today, it is very easy for someone to find your birthday or your anniversary date. I am a strong advocate that on social media (this can be an entire book unto itself) you should not have your correct birth date or year, nor your correct anniversary date or other milestones, posted on the internet for all to see. The less personal information you put about yourself online, the better. How many really go through the security settings to make sure only their friends can see it and not friends of friends, etc.? I consider myself a pretty intelligent guy, and I still can only understand about five percent of all the Google and Facebook settings.

I came up with a fix for this delivery scam. What you can do is you can take an envelope, put $3 to $5 in it, write "tip" on it in black marker, and keep it under the welcome mat at your front door. So, if someone delivers a flower arrangement or candy on a milestone day, you can say, "Leave it on the front porch (or the stairs) and there's a tip for you under the mat" (should you feel obligated to leave a tip). You should then look through the window or the peephole, make sure the delivery person gets back in the vehicle, and they completely pull away before you open the door to retrieve the gift. This can be a lifesaving tip.

The next thing I'd like to talk about is in-home security alarm systems. Many alarm systems give the owners a false sense of security. An alarm system is a great early line of defense, as is having a dog in the house (and that's something we'll discuss later). Many people do not set their alarms because they become a nuisance, they become complacent, or the thing will go off in the middle of the night as a false alarm, so they won't set it anymore.

As noted earlier, you need to figure out the bugs in your system so that it works for you! Reevaluate as needed. The practice of not using your alarm is a very bad thing. You should have an alarm and you should arm it every night. It's not a bad practice to set your alarm as soon as you come home as well. There are ruses, though. Buy some alarm stickers and put them on your windows. This will turn away most amateurs, because they'll feel you do have an alarm. Same thing is done with camera stickers—you know, "warning: 24-hour surveillance" or fake cameras being mounted. A real pro can tell the difference, so don't think it's a good suit of armor that will carry you through all circumstances.

Alarm systems are very sophisticated today. There are many do-it-yourself alarms and stick-em-up wireless internet alarms. The technology is not there yet. 1 believe that these are all substandard. You want a good old-fashioned professionally installed alarm system by a licensed, bonded, insured alarm company. You want central station monitoring. You want a radio back-up mounted in your attic, not just relying on a phone line or a Wi-Fi signal. Keypads should be installed in points of entry of the house, and a great tip is to install a keypad in the master bedroom. Some systems today are changing, where they rely on a cellular signal to make the broadcast to the alarm company. Know the limitations of systems like that, do some research, and make your own conclusions.

The reason I like the keypad in the master bedroom is, when I go to bed at night, if I forgot to set the alarm, I can set it right from the comfort of my bedroom. The other reason I like to have it there is because, if the alarm goes off at three in the morning, I can glance at the keypad in the master bedroom and see where the breach occurred, whether it's the rear sliding glass door, basement window, or a motion detector inside the house. Motion detectors inside the house can often be set off by Mylar balloons, which are given as gifts or brought home from a birthday party. When the heat or air conditioning kicks on, the balloons sway back and forth, and they set the motion detectors off. This is something you should be aware of.

I have recently upgraded to Alarm.com, and all of the controls are on my mobile devices. It is like having a portable keypad and alert center. I still have the traditional keypads in my house as well. I am still not ready to go fully digital. Think about this: Most good alarm systems have two buttons that you can press that will put them in panic mode, set off the alarm, and send a signal to central station. It's good planning to have a keypad in the master bedroom and, if practical, other locations in the home. It is also not a bad idea to have an old hard-wired phone in your house. If you have a low-end handset, it will work when there is no electricity. The alarm installer can also use the line for central station communication as a backup to the battery-operated radio transmitter they install in the attic.

What I also have on my home alarm system is what's known as an "ambush code," or "duress code." An ambush code is something that was originated by jewelry stores. The scenario is, you're going to walk in your house, and someone approaches you from behind and puts a weapon to your back and says, "Open the door and shut off the alarm!" Or they do a push-in as you're entering the home. Well, if your alarm code was 1-2-3-4, for instance, you can program a panic code like 4-3-2-1. That will shut the alarm off and send an ambush code to the central station, which means they will not call your house but instead immediately dispatch the police. The police will be notified that an ambush or duress code was sent back to central monitoring, and that it was a silent alarm that was received. I believe it's a must to have a panic-mode set up in your home alarm system.

With today's fancy alarm systems that can be remotely operated, many of them can be disarmed right from your phone. Now it might seem appealing and convenient to disarm your alarm as soon as you pull into your driveway, but don't do it. Understanding the demands of life today, you might be arriving home with a load of groceries and a toddler. You're juggling things and life all at once. What, and now you have to disarm your alarm once you get inside? That will create more trips! What's the point of this fancy alarm that I can disable remotely if I don't utilize it? Yes, disarm your alarm from inside the house at the main panel. Why? So you can lean on your ambush or duress code should the previous scenario play out. Otherwise, you've removed a crucial tool from your toolbox: no alarm.

I've taken my alarm system one step further. I have a few portable panic buttons, three to be exact. Two I have mounted in areas of the house where we spend the most time as a family unit. One is on a ball-chain necklace, so if I'm out and about the house, on the deck barbecuing, or doing work in the basement, I wear it. Some people will look at that, especially guys, and frown upon it like, "Oh, what a world we live in today!" But I would rather have too much coverage than not enough coverage. This is part of what I call my "belt and suspenders" mentality, the idea being that my pants are not going to fall down…Ensure you have all your bases covered, and give yourself multiple options to notify help when needed.

As discussed earlier, some alarm companies will allow secondary and even tertiary numbers to be on the call list in the event of an alarm. While having too many numbers for the central monitoring station to call can cost valuable time, there are benefits to adding your cellphone, work number, and/or other adult inhabitants' numbers to the list. If there is, in fact, some sort of a home invasion and you are unable to get to the primary phone in your home, you will have another chance to communicate with central monitoring about your situation. In today's society, the "land-line" is fading away, as most people use cell phones. But if you do have a land line or your primary cellphone is not readily available, maybe your domestic partner's phone is, and you'll be able to talk with the alarm company. If you are not home and get a call to a secondary number, you can at least tell the company no one is home and that yes, the police should be dispatched. That will give you a heads up that something might be wrong at the house.

Alarm companies use passwords. When they call in on an alarm, they'll ask who you are and what your password is. If you're being held during a violent invasion, you should not give the password to them, or you should purposefully give them the wrong password. In giving the wrong password, you could follow up with "yes, everything is okay here. It's a false alarm," and the police would be dispatched, with your aggressor not being the wiser. Password selection should be unique to you and your family members. Not something easily guessed. These passwords should not be given out to anyone outside your very close circle of trusted people, usually just the inhabitants of the home. Don't call the alarm company yourself, wait for them to call you. If they are calling you while you are calling them, it might go to your voicemail. While waiting for the police, especially on a false alarm, have some form of identification ready because they most likely will not know that you are the homeowner.

One person I know forgot to turn their alarm off one Saturday morning and decided to take their child outside to play. They had just installed their alarm system somewhat recently, and this whole process was still new to them. The door they decided to use to go outside was not on a timer delay, and the alarm went off immediately, scaring the hell outta both the parent and child. They disarmed the alarm and got a call from the alarm company, "What's the password?" Their mind went blank. They forgot the password, told them they were the homeowner, and the alarm company said the police were on their way. When the police got there, they found the homeowner and their kid playing in the back yard and checked their identification. This was in a middle-class suburban township in New Jersey and it did take about six minutes for the police to come. On one hand, it's bad to have "false" alarms like these, as you can get fined should you have too many. On the other, this was a win. Exactly what was supposed to happen happened. The alarm company called, the password was wrong, and the police showed up.

Another friend of mine has alarm sensors on his gun safe. When the alarm system is set to "stay" or "home" mode, it allows the occupants to move about the house without setting off any motion sensors, and you can also disable sensors on certain doors that you'd normally want protected but may want to go through when your alarm system is set. This particular system was set up so that not only was the sensor one that would go off should the safe be opened, but it would also go off if the safe were to be tipped over. Because of this design, that sensor would be "hot" any time the alarm was armed. On more than one occasion, my friend would be getting ready in the morning before heading to the range and forget to disarm the alarm. He's gotten several calls from the alarm company asking for that password and making sure that everything was alright. Again, this is a win. The system is doing what it is supposed to, and he's had an impromptu audit of the alarm company. Be mindful that if you name your safe something like "gun safe," that information will be available to the police and, if there were a situation involving that sensor, they may try to dig around in your firearms, just on the premise that you have them. Keep those implications in mind.

In the same vein of these false alarms testing the system, most alarm systems and companies allow users to put them into "testing" mode. While in testing mode, a homeowner can go through all the sensors with the alarm company, to make sure they are all working properly and signals are being communicated the way they are supposed to. This should be done on a monthly basis.

A final note on alarm systems. If you are in a situation where you have a housekeeper, or perhaps you are having work done at your house and a contractor needs to gain entry, you can program temporary codes. Some systems are sophisticated and will allow you to do all of this right from your mobile device, as is the case with my Alarm.com system. Other systems may have to be programed from the central panel. The usefulness of this is endless. You may want to have a temporary password for a babysitter that is coming over. Perhaps you have a friend or family member watching your house while you are away. Once the need for these people to have access to your home is no longer valid, you can delete the code.

If you don't have an alarm system, a good practice is to keep your car keys nearby. Should a situation happen where someone is trying to gain entry to your home, or you suspect a prowler is on your property, you can set off the panic mode on your car. Not only will the panic alarm on the car potentially scare off any unwanted house guests, it'll also inform your neighbors that something is going on. You know how nosy neighbors can be; they will probably take a look outside themselves, and this is an opportunity to have another witness to help identify any unsavory persons lurking around the neighborhood.

The hardening of your exterior doors should be done in your home. The gross majority of break-ins to homes occur through such an entrance. Reinforced door jams and lock striker plates should be used. The striker plates should be installed with long screws that anchor them in place better than the short, cheap screws that come in most consumer lock sets from your run-of-the-mill home improvement store. Have a high-quality door as well. If you have a standard peephole, replace it with a wide angle one. Consider getting a doorbell camera. They are a great way to see who is at your door, and you can communicate through them. They can also be programed to be motion activated, and most of them will allow footage to be stored in cloud storage. If you do get one, get a high-quality one in high definition.

Quality locks and doorknobs are also important to safeguard your front door. There are also fancy electronic locks that you can get today. Some of them have keypads where you can program a number combination to get in. Other systems are more sophisticated and can connect to Wi-Fi, allowing users to lock, unlock, and check the status remotely. Finally, there are electronic locks that are z-wave radio technology. They would operate the same way, allowing users to remotely control them, but they have the additional benefit of being paired with home automation systems and/or alarm systems that are also equipped with this technology. Remember that temporary password you gave your babysitter? Well, you can also give your housekeeper a temporary entrance code for your front door. Better yet, if you have a lock that is remotely operated through Wi-Fi or z-wave, you can open the door for them when they arrive from, say, your office. Some systems allow specific time frames for when certain codes can be used. Just program your lock for the hour or hour and a half that someone is over, and then, after that period, access denied.

Here is one thing to beware of that I have heard used a few times. If you ever come home and your key does not fit into the lock, you should immediately back away, get to safety, and call the police. There are some savvy thieves that, after they gain access to your place, will stick a toothpick with crazy glue on it into the tumbler of the lock and break off the excess. They do this so that, if anyone arrives home while they are in the middle of looting, they have a heads-up warning of you trying to enter, and they can escape out the back or from a window.

Normal house keys with ridges on one side are a liability, and their locks can easily be opened with Bump Keys. Most modern locks can be defeated in a matter of seconds. You can buy them online and at many flea markets. With a few minutes watching YouTube videos, you can see how easily they work. This is why all entry doors should have either keycode locks or additional blind

If your front door lock is compromised, walk away immediately.

CrimeProofBook.com

deadbolt locks on the inside of the door, with no key option on the front of the door.

Front doors are the most common entry point burglars use to gain entry into homes; windows on the first floor are the second most common. Make sure you keep your windows locked. If you do have an alarm system, have glass break alarms and window sensors installed. There is one product on the market that is really a game changer when it comes to window security, and it's called CJ Buffer Security Film. This material comes in a variety of different thicknesses and is applied right onto your window. It is see-through and impact resistant. The level of protection you have depends on the thickness of material you get. The lower-level protection will make it difficult for someone to beat in and break the glass. The thicker varieties are bullet and explosion proof. What a game changer this is! You can use this on glass doors, regular windows, and side-of-door windows for added protection. The material is not inexpensive, but it is well worth it.

The next thing I want to discuss with home security is garage door protection. I've learned over the years from garage door installers, alarm companies, and police that this is a serious breach point for home robberies. Most people that have attached garages never lock the door between the garage and the house, and this makes for an easy entry point for a robbery. With most old-fashioned

Most modern locks can be defeated.

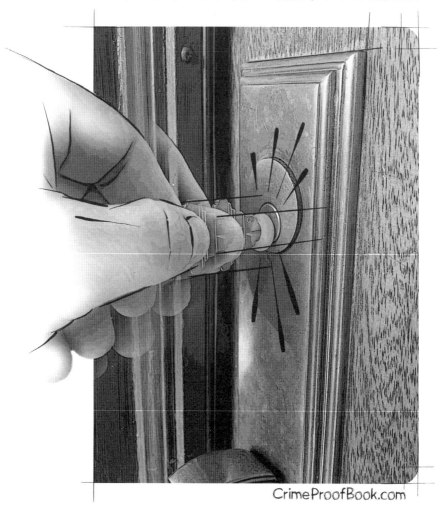

CrimeProofBook.com

overhead garage doors, if you were to take a bumper-jack from a car manufactured up until the 90s and put it under the lip of the garage door and jack it up, you would bend the two roller frames into the ceiling, giving enough room for the bad guy to slide under and get inside your garage. Once inside your garage, they can work on opening the door to the house, unless, of course, like most people, the door is unlocked.

Another thing to be aware of concerning garage doors—by law, every electric garage door opener has to have that little red string with a red barb hanging from the rail on the garage door system. This is because, if you were exiting the garage during a power failure, you could disconnect the door from the track and you could open the door manually. I had an alarm installer give me a tip; they caught a crew of guys in Southern Jersey who were using a cordless drill and a four inch hole saw to cut a hole in the door. They would drill into the center of your garage door and pull the red string down, allowing them to open the garage door, gaining entry to your garage. They could close the garage door behind them, stick the hole back into the spot where they cut it out, and now they have security and safety. They're cloaked behind your door while they sift through the stuff in your garage or get to work on that entrance door to your home. They can also purchase a professional Garage Lock Bypass Tool, which is sold online for under $30. This tool is pushed past the weather-stripping at the top of the garage door,

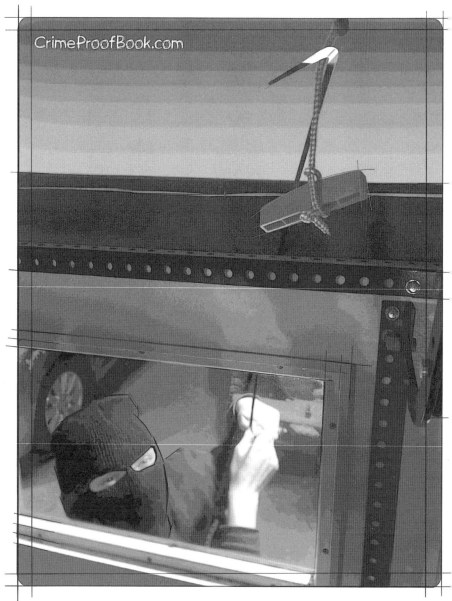

They're cloaked behind your door while
they sift through the stuff in your garage.

hooks the safety release, and allows you to open the garage door with ease.

Of course, many older garage door panels can be kicked in to gain entry the same way.

Most people will program their garage door openers that are built into their car, or will keep a remote in their car. They won't lock their car doors when parked in the driveway. You're serving entrance to your garage on a silver platter when you don't lock your car doors and have remote abilities to open it in the vehicle. It is also very easy for a burglar to smash a window on your car and press the garage door opener, so those remotes should be hidden.

The best thing you can do if you're replacing your garage doors is install solid-panel garage doors with no windows in them, and have your installer put in jack shaft motors. These motors mount on the side of a garage door. They cannot be forced open, there's no track to crush in the ceiling, and the override button is right on the jack shaft motor on the side of the garage door. It's almost impossible for a thief to gain entry forcefully through a system like that.

The other thing to do to harden your garage is have a real solid-core door between the house and the garage. In most municipalities, it is code to have a fire-rated door between the garage and the dwelling where people live, and you should have a good commercial lock and a deadbolt that are always locked.

You should get into your car and lock the door before you open the garage whenever you are leaving the house, and the reverse when arriving home. It is very easy for someone to enter the garage while it is opening or closing and surprise you at this vulnerable moment.

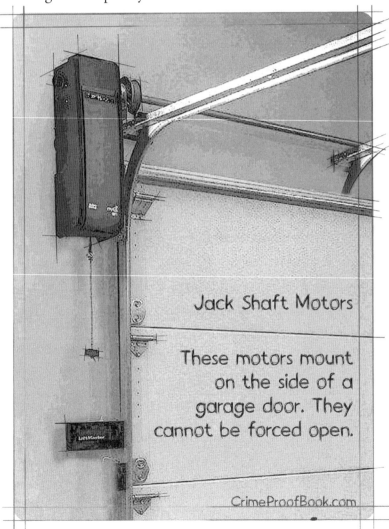

Jack Shaft Motors

These motors mount on the side of a garage door. They cannot be forced open.

CrimeProofBook.com

While we're on the subject of home security, I mentioned earlier that a dog is a great first line of security. I don't care if your dog is three pounds or 300 pounds, if that dog senses strangers, barks, and makes noise, it's a great alarm system. But dogs are not for everybody. With people's lifestyles, (e.g., husband and wife both working, nobody home to care for the dog, etc.), I realize that it's a big commitment. There are little smoke and mirror tactics that can be utilized. One of them would be, outside the house, put a couple of big dog dishes and a couple of dog toys. Maybe put some inside the kitchen where, if someone was to look through a sliding glass door or the kitchen window, they would see the dishes and toys. This might make them think twice about attempting to gain entry into your house. The thief would not be sure if you have a 200-pound Rottweiler sitting around waiting for them if they come into the house, a yipping mop dog, or in this case no dog at all. This can work. This is another defensive tool that you can use just by giving the image that you have a dog in the house when, in fact, you don't. Something to note: there are doorbells on the market that, when you press them, sound like a dog barking. I don't like them. Even your common idiot can understand that they're fake. Every time they press the doorbell, it's the same sound they hear. People think that's going to do the job. That's not going to do the job.

Other things you can do to create illusions in your home are using lights on timers. Maybe you come home from work late or work overnight. Maybe you're away for the weekend. Whatever the scenario, using light timers can give the illusion that someone is home. Program the timers so lights will go on and off at different times in your home. Make it seem like you're on the first floor, maybe in the living room, for one portion of the evening. Then have that light turn off and, after some time, have one turn on in the bedroom. Play around with this idea and try to pattern a normal evening if you're not going to be around or come home really late. Those new home automation systems that use Wi-Fi or z-wave may have outlets that you can program right from your mobile device. Some systems will allow you to program random times between a certain time frame for lights to be energized. The tools are out there. A cool device that does the same thing is a fake TV box. These are electric light-emitting boxes that project randomized light patterns on a wall. From the outside of a home at night, it'll appear as if a TV is on in a certain room, as the light can be seen through and around certain window treatments. Set those on timers too!

Even though this is automotive-related, it does tie into home security. Most people have GPS systems either built into their car or a portable one, and they don't use a password to lock them. Well, here's a scam that was going on in a major mall in New Jersey: if you let your car be valet parked, always use a split key ring. Everyone should have a two-piece key ring, and you should only give the valet your car key, not your other personal keys. Think of this: When the valet parker would park the car, he or she would open the glove box and look for the registration or the insurance card with the home address. I teach all of my students to take anything with your address—registration, insurance cards, anything else—put them in a zip-lock bag, and put them under the floor mat of the back seat.

If the valet parker cannot retrieve your address from documents, he will turn your GPS on and press "home" to gain your address. He has a friend who's parked in the valet lot in a white van. Inside the white van is a key cutting machine. Since it is nearly impossible to duplicate and replicate an automotive key because of microchip technology, etc., they will write down on an envelope your address that they retrieved from either your registration, insurance, or GPS, and they will cut every key on the key ring that they have blanks for and put them in the envelope. That is a very valuable package on the criminal market. They will either break into your house themselves or they will sell the package to someone to break into your house. My advice, again, is to have documentation in a zip-lock bag under a floor mat and your GPS program for home actually going to the address of the nearest police

Only give the valet your car key.

department to your house. Imagine the two criminals, two in the morning on their way to your house with keys to break in, and it takes them right to the driveway of the police department in your local town. You should also keep an inventory as to how many keys you have.

This is a serious concept, and we should teach all of our family members to do it. "HOME" should not be programmed as home. Either use the address of a local police department, or use the address of someone 20 doors down from you. But I don't really like that idea too much because they might have written down the model of your car and they'll see it in the driveway. Criminals are not stupid; they're just lazy. They might have also written down your plate number, so as they're driving down the block, they see your black jeep with the matching plate number, BINGO! They have keys to it. Remember:

(1) Two-piece pull apart key ring

(2) Change "home" on your GPS

(3) Secure your registration, insurance cards, and any other correspondence that you have.

I had a gentleman take a Bentley to my class, a $300,000 Bentley. In the back seat, he had all of his mail. He and his wife went to dinner using valet parking. The next day, his house was broken into. When they caught the guys, they said they got the address from the mail on the back seat. They couldn't copy the Bentley key because it was an electronic key. But they copied all the other keys on his ring because he did not have a split-key ring. These are great lessons to learn and live by.

While you're contemplating the security of your home, don't forget the outside. Do you have a shed with gardening tools in it? Is the shed locked? Are there items in there that will make a crook's job easier to gain entry into your home? Think about those items. Don't keep ladders outside, thinking they are out of the way, leaning horizontally against the side of the house. That's an invitation for them to be used to get into a second story window. If you have no place to store a ladder, chain it to something so it cannot be used against you. Do you have a couple of old bricks or cinder blocks laying around for some project? Those are master keys to glass doors. Look around the exterior of your home and remove anything that will give the criminals the upper hand. Utilize motion activated flood lights. Noted earlier, consider getting doorbell cams and add to that list flood light cams. These are great devices that can let you see what is going on without having to go outside or even be at home! Many of those cam systems have two-way communications, and some of them have high-decibel alarms you can remotely set off – you've seen the commercials!

As you can see, the idea of hardening your home and employing home safety tactics can have a lot involved. Take into consideration the concepts discussed in this chapter and survey your home for potential weakness. Set yourself up for success! There should be thinking involved as well as discussions with those you live with. Further, these awareness ideas can be applied elsewhere in your life, as you hone your Defensive Mindset.

CHAPTER
05

Protecting Yourself Outside the Home

Where are you more likely to be attacked? At home, where you have the advantage of knowing all the ins and outs, or while you're away from home, going on about your business? The success one has in defending themselves in their home is stacked in favor of the occupants of that home if they're prepared. There are a lot of things you can control while having this home court advantage. When you're away from your castle, that is when the number of variables outside of your control goes up dramatically. That is not to say you cannot protect yourself or be prepared, it's simply why it's all the more important to adopt a Defensive Mindset.

Other chapters in this book are going to focus more on specific situations outside the home. Some of those include while traveling, dealing with an active shooter situation, while at work, or while living at a higher education institute. Concepts and ideas from this chapter can be injected into all of those scenarios, as can ideas outlined in, say, the travel chapter—they all have worth in your day-to-day life. The material all goes hand in hand to better add to the Defensive Mindset. Pick, choose, and use as you desire.

Automobile safety and getting to where you're going by car

The biggest, or rather most prevalent, category of safety-related topics outside the home is going to be dealing with vehicles. Unless you live in a big city and have no car or use for a car, the majority of the people who are going to embark into the world when they leave their home will do so in a personal vehicle. Rideshare, taxi, train, and airplane/airport tips will be included in the travel chapter.

Because this book is more about preparedness for the unknown, I'm not going to put a large emphasis on the condition of your particular vehicle. I will say, though, make sure you keep up with the required maintenance on it, have proper tire pressure, keep that fuel tank more than 50%, and make sure you have a safe and reliable ride. Follow up with any recalls that your car, truck, SUV, or van may have, and do your best to keep warranties active, should you have any.

Remember those tips and tricks discussed when dealing with valet parking and keeping anything personally identifying out of your vehicle? In the shopping safety chapter, I'm going to talk about keeping a dark colored blanket in your car. This is not only good for keeping you warm should you need it during a breakdown or other purpose, but you can also use it to cover up items in your vehicle that prying eyes may want to see. I like to use window tinting on my cars. Most cars today have some level of window tint. Should yours not, consider tinting the back and rear windows. Keep in mind some states have strict window tinting laws: follow them. There is no reason to attract additional attention to you from the police, which can lead to other fishing expeditions by them. One of my loyal Gun For Hire alumni, George Olschewski, who listens to my radio show, suggested this:

"Completely agree with the blanket in the car, and I'll explain why. In winter, way, way too many of us go outside wearing relatively light clothing despite the weather, because we use our cars as a coat. We're in and out of our house, the store, the mall, etc. and we figure, 'Oh, it's only for a minute,' until we get into a car wreck, run out of gas, or some other event where the car won't run. Now, you're cold, uncomfortable, and depending on where you are, the time of day, and weather conditions, who knows when help will show up? If you're going to wear your car like a coat, PLEASE have sufficient things with you to keep you warm!"

Other key items to keep in your car should include a spare tire, jack, and lug wrench. If you buy or procure a new or new-to-you car, check these items out. Make sure they work, and all the pieces are together. Go through a tire change dry run to make sure you'll be able to do this should you need to. If you don't know how to change a tire, learn. A friend of mine found out a car he bought brand new did not have a lug wrench when he was on the side of the road attempting to change a flat tire. Since then, he keeps with his spare tire one of those four-way lug wrenches, not only to give more leverage to him if he needs to change a tire, but he has also used it to aid other motorists that did not have a lug wrench and the lug nuts were different than the ones he had on his car (most lug wrenches included with your basic jack are cheesy; make sure you are physically able to use them). Being able to change your own tire goes beyond basic self-sufficiency. When you're broken down on the side of the road, you are vulnerable to being targeted by people with ill intent. If it's safe to and you're able to change your own tire, the quicker you can get back on the road, all the better.

Besides tire-changing gear, a small and basic tool kit could come in handy. You may not be a master mechanic, but a problem you have in your life might not be with your car, and the tools you carry may allow you to solve it. Things like pocketknives and multi-tools are handy to get you out of a bind. Consider keeping a seatbelt cutter within arm's reach

of the driver's seat. Duct tape, emergency foil blankets, toilet paper, a small travel air compressor, a tire pressure gauge, an ice scraper, and emergency flares/light are all worth their weight in gold if needed. If you don't carry a high lumen flashlight on your person, keep one in your car close to the driver's seat. More on that flashlight later.

All of those ideas concerning preparedness while in or using your vehicle need to be considered.

There are many scams and crimes committed on our roads, and even though you feel safe in your vehicle, there are some precautions we can take to minimize our chances of becoming a victim. I will start out by saying that every vehicle in your household should have an emergency roadside kit, including items mentioned above, especially if you have children away at college. As a parent, make sure your child has a roadside assistance program for their car. It is also not a bad thing to teach them how to perform basic checks and maintenance as well.

Trained professional criminals are always honing their craft, and we need to be aware that there are always new scams.

A popular scam, especially in urban areas, is the "bump and rob." It works like this. You are stopped at a light and another car bumps you from the rear. You get out to investigate, you are robbed, and possibly your car is jacked as well! If you are bumped by another car, survey the area and stay in the car with the doors locked and the windows up. Just crack the driver's side window to be able to communicate with the other driver if needed. Immediately call the police and report the accident. If you must pull the car over out of the road for safety, make sure you have a clear path forward in case you have to get away quickly. Do not box the front of your vehicle in. If the police are delayed, you can exchange information with the other driver without exiting your vehicle. After the exchange, you can drive to a safe location and survey the damage, if any. If you are in a town you are not familiar with, drive to the nearest police station lot. This is one of the safest areas. Police departments have police entering and exiting the building as well as cameras everywhere, and the criminals know that.

This scenario is one of the most important reasons I always stress that your cell phone is fully charged, and you are never traveling with less than a half a tank of gas. If your vehicle dies, try to move over to the shoulder as far to the side as possible. Every year you hear about motorists getting hit from the rear when disabled on the side of the road. If it is winter and the vehicle still runs, you will thank me for having enough gas in the car so you can keep it running without freezing to death. If the car experiences a catastrophic failure and your electrical system dies, you will also thank me for having a fully charged cell phone.

Immediately call a family member and report your location and problem. Next you should call your roadside service company and report your location, etc. I am a huge advocate of roadside service companies, and I purchase them for all my loved ones as gifts every year. If you are on a highway, do NOT step into the road to be a "mechanic." This is a sure way to get hit by another car. Over 4000 people per year are killed standing outside their vehicle.

Sit in the vehicle, flashers on and at that point, to conserve battery life on your cell phone, shut off Wi-Fi and

Bluetooth. This will greatly extend battery life. Don't sit there playing a game on your phone or scour through social media posts! Save your battery. Make sure your seatbelt is on at all times as well.

While waiting for help, it is best to stay in your vehicle the entire time. A trick that you can use is to move to the passenger seat if you are alone. If you are accidentally struck from behind you will not meet the steering wheel at 60 miles per hour, and if a strange person approaches to offer help, you can crack the window open and tell them the driver went with a police officer for help and they will be right back! Plenty of people have been robbed, raped, and/or assaulted by "good Samaritans" stopping to offer help. Keep in mind, serial killer Ted Bundy used to pretend to be a police officer or other first responder to get his victims to lower their guard, as well as pretending to be an injured person. Don't let the next Ted Bundy prey on you!

Although carjacking is rare, you must remain vigilant when driving. One of the biggest tips I can offer is to always stop in traffic, making sure that you can see the rear tires of the vehicle in front of you. This will allow you to be able to pull out in an emergency situation. If you pull too close to the car in front of you, you can be boxed in if a car pulls too close behind you. You also need to be especially vigilant in high-crime areas where someone can approach your vehicle with a gun and rob you and/or your car. Keep the doors locked, the windows locked, and your head on a swivel whenever stopping. There may be times you are put in an uncomfortable position where someone stands in the front of your car and demands you get out! I know what I would do if put in that position, but not everyone can make that same decision. These are things you need to think about before they happen. If you are approached by a carjacker with or without a weapon and you fear for your life, let them have the car but at all costs do not let them abduct you!

There is no such thing as a routine traffic stop! You may think you are being pulled over for something insignificant like failing to yield or a broken brake light, when in fact you and your vehicle may meet the description of someone who just completed a violent felony. You are in the wrong place at the wrong time.

When pulling over, choose an area that is safe for you and the officer, as close to the shoulder as possible. At this point you should shut off the car and remove the key if it has a physical key. This is important to show the officer that you are not planning a quick getaway. The next thing you should do is open both front windows and if the rear windows are tinted open them all as well. This will allow the approaching officer full visibility of the occupants in the car. Now is not the time to reach in your purse or hip pocket to retrieve your credentials. You should also not dig around in the console or the glove compartment. Imagine the perspective of the officer as he is approaching your vehicle and you look like you are reaching for something or trying to hide something! Remain seated upright with your hands on the steering wheel until the officer approaches.

Once the officer approaches, follow their command for ID, etc. It is at this point that you explain to the officer where your credentials are and wait for them to tell you to retrieve them, and do it slowly. Ask for permission to get your wallet out of your pocket. If you have any type of police support cards, you should hand them to the officer with your other documents now. After you supply your credentials, put your hands back on the steering wheel while they run a background check. While the officer is back at the car, remember that that's not the time to reach for your cell phone and start texting people. Remember the optics from the officer's perspective. Make sure you do not seem like a threat to any police officer. I call this the Labrador posture. Think of a Labrador Retriever rolling over on his back, showing his belly to be rubbed. Show the officer you're a good person. Be a Labrador as long as you're not undercutting your rights. I find the most effective tactic for getting out of a ticket is being respectful with the officer. Remember, they are usually just doing their job, and a roadside pullover is a stressful time for them as well. If you are videoing the entire stop from your phone, it may create an adversarial situation as well.

In a state like New Jersey, where our self-defense options are severely limited, many people tell me they keep a baseball bat in their car. My response is, "You'd better have a mitt and a ball as well." Your lawyer will thank you. Fact of the matter is, you are much safer legally if you have a protection item that is, in fact, automotive related. If you are a carpenter by trade and you have a hammer in the car, you better have nails and a tool belt as well. There are many scenarios where someone exited their car and used a tool, a pipe, or a bat for self-defense. Remember the optics if you use these types of devices. The media will have a field day and the prosecutor will look to villainize you even further than they were already intending to.

What I recommend to all my students is they get a Maglite. These flashlights are made in America, they now have LED bulbs, and are made of a full aluminum body. You can have a four, five, or six D or C battery Maglite in your car

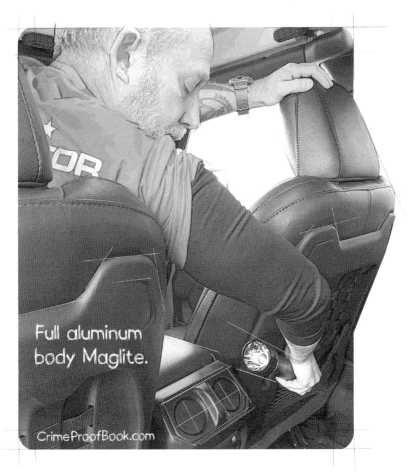

Full aluminum body Maglite.

CrimeProofBook.com

legally because it is an emergency device. Beyond having the Mag lite for its intended purpose, it is also good for temporarily blinding someone as they approach you with bad intentions. What makes this a self-defense possibility is, it can be used as a striking object as well. You get all the benefit without the negative ramifications of carrying a "weapon." They make great gifts and stocking stuffers for all your family and loved ones. More on weapons to come in another chapter.

You've gotten to where you're going – General outside the home protections

We've explored the importance of keeping yourself safe in your car and during your journey, but what about once you've arrived on location? The awareness concepts talked about in the preceding chapters can and should be applied here as well. Again, add to your corporeal knowledge base to develop the Defensive Mindset.

There are threats everywhere and you need to lean on your awareness to help thwart them. Just because you have not had a bad encounter does not mean you won't. Places like shopping malls and parking garages will be discussed a bit more in other chapters, but they need to be looked at in general terms first.

Parking lots and, more specifically, parking garages are big liabilities to your safety. The most obvious is getting hit by a vehicle. If you've got children with you, you must keep on top of them when navigating any parking facility. Due to their usually short height, many motorists that are backing up may not see them. Keep them close. If you have things to get out of your car upon arrival, have your child stand close to the car with their hand on it. Perhaps use the gas fill cover plate as a reference point. You can also purchase a number of neat magnets to put in specific areas to have your child put their hand. Some are marketed specifically for this purpose. The goal here is to condition your kids to not wander through a parking lot.

Have your child stand close to the car and touch a reference point.

With most cars that have remote unlocking, one button press will unlock the driver's side and two button presses will unlock all the doors. When approaching your car, if there is no reason to unlock all the doors, only unlock the driver's side. Do not get into the habit of always double clicking the remote, leaving you vulnerable to having someone pop into the passenger side or a rear door.

Parking lots and garages offer a good amount of concealment and cover to criminals. It's not difficult to hide on the other side of a car or even under a big SUV. You must keep your head on a swivel and maintain a good level of awareness in these locations. Garages are particularly dangerous for numerous reasons. They may not be well lit, provide a good level of cover and concealment (concrete pillars), and have limited egress from the general area. Their cloaked nature makes them specifically a good place to prey on victims. Mall parking lots are also notorious for carjackings. The more brazen ones are now taking place at valet parking areas, and I have also seen carjackings at the carwash after the car is cleaned.

You're going to have many different destinations as you go on about your daily life. Those destinations can include small mom and pop stores, strip malls, sports arenas, theme parks, big box stores, so on and so forth. Maybe your errands are going to be run on foot, after you parked, and you need to walk from location to location. That is when you must keep yourself in Condition Yellow. Head on a swivel, scanning the area, and making non-aggressive eye contact with any passerby.

It is not a bad idea to also have a lifeguard whistle on your person as well to draw attention if the need arises.

If you find yourself in a situation where you are going from Condition Yellow to Condition Orange, use the most effective defensive weapon you have. Your feet. The best way to defend yourself from an aggressor is to completely avoid one. If something does not seem right, it probably is not right. Walk in another direction and, if you find that you are being followed, you may have to run. Popping into a crowded store or establishment could be all you need to do to evade someone with ill intent. Yeah, you can be boxing yourself into that location, but the bigger, louder, and more different you can make yourself from your surroundings, the better (on the street, in a store, wherever). Barging into a bustling coffee shop that is pumping out lattes may give you an edge, especially if you get followed in, and start screaming "fire." Why fire? Because that's an immediate danger to everyone in that location and bound to grab attention – bigger, louder, and different than your surroundings! Hopefully that will ward off whoever is following you and/or have people standing by to offer aid (although in this day and age, you're liable to be greeted by several cell phones filming your interaction versus intervening in it).

Banking

With the convenience of online banking today, some people rarely have to go to a physical bank location. That's not to say people don't go to banks, but it's so easy to check account statuses, transfer money, pay bills, and even deposit checks all from your computer or mobile device. That being said, there are just some things that need to be done at the bank, or hey, some of us won't give up old habits and prefer face-to-face interactions. Going to a bank has not been completely phased out.

A big thing you should avoid is going to an ATM in the middle of the night, or any time, really. I use the ATM only as a very last resort. But going in the middle of the night is a sure way to become a target. If you do have to go to an ATM, don't leave your receipt lying around. Don't leave it at the ATM or in your car, especially if you're going to valet park. Save it in your house. Periodically, you should burn your sensitive mail or buy a shredder. The best thing is to shred whatever you don't need as soon as you get it, so it does not pile up.

Also concerning ATMs, you need to be hyper aware of what is going on around you. The ATMs that are fully enclosed may give you a sense of security, but in reality, they are little crime bubbles where, if someone gets inside with you, they can have a field day with you. And no one may be around to help. Keep this in mind.

When it comes to going to a bank, make sure the blank deposit or withdrawal slips are legitimate ones. People have been known to reprint deposit slips with different routing numbers, which will deposit the money right into their bank account, and put those slips in the places where the bank stores blank ones. It's best to use deposit slips that come with your checks. Then you can be sure all the numbers are right.

In the late 80s and 90s, a lot of banks started to phase out armed guards. Why did this happen? Armed guards turned into liabilities for the banks because they would be the first ones shot during a robbery. Their answer was to remove the liability of having to pay families for deceased loved ones. Look around the bank you go to—ever see armed guards? Probably not. How do I know this? Because a friend of mine's father who worked in a large banking institute had a big box of old service holsters that were given out when they phased out such guards. This was a conscientious decision that was made, and made to protect the banks, not you, the customer. Should an armed robbery occur when you're at a bank, you're on your own! I suggest that you do not be the hero. Keep your head down and comply.

Hospital patient security

It is no shock that hospital patients are vulnerable. You may have been there before too. Strange environment, drugs to relax or incapacitate you, room doors wide open, and shared with more than one person. Hospital staff in and out 24 hours a day. When you or a loved one is admitted to the hospital, it is imperative that, as soon as possible, all personal items are taken home. Property theft is the number one crime committed in hospitals. The only items a patient should have are their electronic device and charger, period!

Assaults are also committed in hospitals, so you must always be aware, have the nurse call button close by, and protect yourself with any means possible—but in reality, the best defense is to try to stay in Condition Yellow when physically possible. It is also important to have a strong showing of support while in the hospital—high visitor traffic and loved ones showing concern and dropping in at off hours are great deterrents. I have used my persuasive powers more than once to visit someone during the non-visitation hours.

Another important thing is to make sure you are or have a good patient advocate. Should it be you that is admitted into the hospital, make sure that your friend or loved one that is involved in your care and status is able to stay connected. The same advice applies for you to be a good patient advocate. Having a direct line number to nursing stations and knowing the times for staff changes are a few things to be aware of. Someone checking in often for updates during prolonged stays also aids in a show of force for whoever is admitted. This will also allow your trusted person(s) stay in the loop.

Different hospitals have different security protocols. The facility and even the entrance one takes to get into the hospital dictates what kind of security checks there may be. For example, one facility has metal detectors and security guards at the entrance to their emergency room waiting area. The same facility that is attached to the rest of the hospital has minimal security at the other entrances. If you have some sort of weapon, such as a knife or pepper spray, be aware that those items might be prohibited on the hospital grounds.

Being subjected to staying in a hospital or visiting a loved one is a stressful situation as it is. If the hospital stay is extended, visitors (and patients) should be aware of the property layout. In general, any emergency egress routes, stairwells, and fire alarm pull stations should all be noted. Make sure you stay protected and don't fall prey to another type of emergency when being in such situations.

Bathrooms

Sexual assaults can happen in bathrooms, especially public ones. When in public, this is something you need to be aware of. If you're at work, work in a big building, and share the restroom on your floor with other companies, you don't know who could be coming into that bathroom.

When you walk into the restroom, look to see who else is in there. Women should always use the stall closest to the door and sink. Don't take the one in the back. The one in the back can often be the handicap stall, which is typically larger. Someone could push you into the stall, lock the door, and proceed to attack you. If this should happen, you must act quickly, loudly, and fight like your life depends on it, because it does. This is a perfect scenario to have mace or pepper spray at the ready.

Women should put their purses around their necks. Listen to who is walking by. Don't have your headphones on in the restroom. You should have your phone out.

Everyone should be aware of cameras in the restroom. A lot more people are using those micro cameras, aka button cams. If you see a pinhole in a drop ceiling, be suspicious. In 2019, there were two high profile cases involving people putting hidden cameras in the restrooms on airplanes. Keep in mind, those are two cases in one year—ones we KNOW about. Always be aware of your surroundings.

When you're done in the bathroom, walk out with purpose. You don't know who could follow you, wait for you to come out, and push you back into the bathroom.

Gentlemen, if you can, use a urinal against the wall in a bathroom, or one near a mirror so you can see who is coming and going behind you. Stand on an angle so you can see who is coming and going. If you're concerned with safety, use the stall rather than a urinal. This is literally the time you'll be caught with your d*ck in your hands if attacked.

Pumping gas, outside bathrooms, and convenience store safety

In New Jersey, we are the last state that does not allow people to pump their own gas. We are spoiled and we get to stay in the vehicle during the entire transaction. Of course, you must also be aware of panhandlers approaching you and possibly distracting you. This is a perfect time for an accomplice to run up and grab your wallet or purse from the front seat because you left the passenger side window open and your valuables on the seat. Keep the window up and only lower it enough to pass your payment through.

That is not the time to leave your vehicle while it is being filled up, leaving your keys, children, or valuables in the car. I always choose for safety reasons to wait until the transaction is complete, then park in the lot. Once parked, I'll go use the restroom or convenience store. I am not a fan of restrooms that are located outside of a service station, especially around the back of the building. This leaves you very vulnerable. When traveling alone or with children, you should only use these restrooms as a last resort. Try to pick locations where the restrooms are inside, where there are employees as well as other customers. Witnesses are the enemy of criminals. Take your young children with you to the bathroom and stay together.

When traveling in the other 49 states, where you have to pump your own gas, I have some safety ideas to take into consideration. Cars have been stolen, some with children in them, because the driver neglected to remove the ignition key and lock the doors! Some cars have the filler cap on the driver's side and some on the passenger side. Be aware of any blind spots as you pull up to the pump. You must make sure you are in Condition Yellow during the entire visit to the gas station. At a gas station, always be aware of whether or not the nozzle is still inserted in your gas tank; if you panic and drive away, you will drag the nozzle and hose off with you (which are designed to break away, but are still full of gasoline).

While we are on this topic, I would like to remind you that one of the most dangerous jobs in the USA is convenience store worker. When I visit a convenience store, I will pull up and sit in my car for 30 seconds and scope out the area to make sure there is nothing abnormal. Is the clerk visible from the window, are there customers exiting and entering? I look to see if there are any vagrants or panhandlers waiting for customers to fleece. How about the obvious, someone holding the place up at gun point? The idea here is to look before you leap and know what you're walking into.

When I enter the store, I am fully aware of all my surroundings and hypersensitive to all the other customers I can see. After I pick up what I need, I scope out the counter and register, then proceed to get in line to pay. The entire time my head is on a swivel, scanning the area. Don't get caught between the robber and the counter person. Many operators of convenience stores have firearms behind the counter. Remember, depending on your jurisdiction, you may have the right to keep a firearm at your place of business. When taking out your money or card to pay, you should not pull out a large wad of cash, even if it is singles. To a criminal this says "jackpot!" After you pay, gather your items and proceed to walk out, maintaining a good view of the exit, front of the store, and the parking lot. Walk to your vehicle with a purpose, unlock the door, enter the car, and lock all the doors when you get in.

A convenience store scenario that I always discuss with my students in an unarmed state like New Jersey is that, if I am ever in a store and an armed robber announces themselves, I would keep my head down slightly, so as not to make eye contact with the bad guy. This may minimize my chances of being killed. I would also be hypervigilant of the surroundings because there might be more than one perpetrator. If it is a routine robbery where you mind your business and keep your head down, then there is a better chance of survival. I mean, hell, if a gun was stuck in my face, I would give up my money. But if the bad guy announces that we are all to get in the back of the store, or he wants us all on the ground, we then have a problem. I will now take my chances by rushing the bad guy. I must note that that decision is NOT for everyone, but I would rather die fighting than complying.

You can see that gas stations, convenience stores, and restrooms located outside of the actual service station or store have a unique set of hazards to be aware of. Be vigilant in these scenarios and never let your guard down!

House of worship security and safety measures

Over the past ten years we have seen a huge spike in attacks on congregants in houses of worship. One of the main reasons is because they are such a soft target. Hundreds of people in one large open room, usually unarmed and with very few defined exits, is a recipe for disaster.

There are tactical decisions you can make to help further protect you and your loved ones in such an environment.

Remember to keep your head on a swivel at all times. Secure a seat(s) close to an exit with a wall or two nearby so you have less of an area to scan. Kind of like having the bad guy funnel into your space. Most houses of worship are made of stone and masonry, so you may find some good cover, if needed. When seated, review all emergency exits and review with your family that, if there was an emergency, those are the closest exits. Condition Yellow is in full force in a house of worship!

You must do the same when entering and exiting the building before and after services. Does everything look right? Does something stand out as different, weird, or out of place? Are there new faces you have never seen before? Do those faces look like they have an agenda other than a spiritual one? In the summer, be aware of anyone wearing bulky or long clothing; they may be concealing a weapon.

Having a security team is essential in this day and age, and there are plenty of resources out there to help you assemble one. This is a MUST!

Remember, if there is an attack, run in a safe direction and do not look back, stay down as low as possible, and seek out any cover or concealment points. Once you have exited, you can use cars as cover if needed until help arrives.

If the attack is on top of you, you may make the decision to "rush the nut." This may be your only option, and I would rather face my attacker and take the odds rather than be shot in the back trying to flee. Again, fight or flight reflexes kick in, and this is NOT for everyone.

No one wants to think about this or have to worry about it when engaged in religious fellowship or spiritual prayer. But, unfortunately, this is a stress that has been thrust upon us as a free society. Like any other place, constant vigilance and attention to what is going on will help safeguard yourself and your family.

How's your tool belt feeling? A bit heavier? I hope so. Read onto the following chapters about guarding yourself from danger in other situations outside the home.

CHAPTER
06

Shopping Safety

We've thoroughly explored that threats to you and your loved ones are prevalent when outside the home. Look at your weekly routine. If you're like most Americans, your time is spent at work, at home, and doing chores and errands. Unless you are a complete shut-in, working from home and relying on grocery and goods delivery services, you leave the house to go shopping. Some of the concepts and ideas in this chapter have been covered already; however, taking a closer look is important to developing your Defensive Mindset. Malls, grocery stores, and other shopping centers are a prime place for predators, out in full force looking for prey. Let's not make it easy for them!

Shopping almost always includes a currency exchange of one form or another. Unless you are the type of person that likes to just window shop, take a look at new gadgets, or see what is for sale, you're probably going to buy something when you're on such shopping expeditions. Some things you can do to protect yourself from seeming like a lucrative target involve the principle of not keeping all of your eggs in one basket.

Keep your identification separate from your cash. Use things like money clips and "smallets" for cash. Something I carry is a wad of cash with a few singles and a $20 bill, the "chump change" trick. If you're getting

"Smallet"

robbed, take out the roll, tell them that's all you have, then throw your "chump change" in a direction opposite to the direction you are planning on fleeing towards.

"Chump change"

CrimeProofBook.com

Avoid carrying large quantities of cash in public, but if you must, keep the big bills separate from your "chump change." You may get robbed and be out of some money, you may even lose your watch and cell phone during this encounter, but at least all of your identification documents will not go down with the ship. Having to get new driver's licenses and similar documents after getting mugged only adds insult to injury.

Avoid carrying large purses or bags that you store your important stuff in. Not only are they cumbersome to navigate with, especially in a Condition Red situation, they are also easy to snatch up. Cull out what is necessary versus not necessary. Go into the world with the preconceived notion that whatever is in such a bag is prime for the taking. So, smaller is better.

Most people today have credit cards. Hey, they are convenient, offer consumer protection, and many companies offer rewards when you use them. Some of those rewards are beneficial to consumers, provided they pay off the balance every month. Let's say you have that one coveted credit card, the one you've had for years, and it has a ten or twenty thousand dollar limit. Bravo. Do you ever charge twenty thousand on a credit card? Most of us don't. Some of us do. I don't know your personal or business dealings, but a credit card with a large spending limit can be a liability to you for multiple reasons.

Leave those cards with the big limits at home, unless you know you're going to need that much spending power. Instead, have cards with smaller limits. Something that seasonal employees may do is "skim your card." They either use a device to collect all the credit card information or outright transcribe all the data on it. Skimming devices can also be put at gas station pumps, so be wary of a credit card slot that looks like it's been tampered with at the pump, or anywhere for that matter. Regardless, should your numbers be skimmed, you'll be dealing with a card with a smaller credit limit. Not only does the smaller limit stop potential thieves from racking up your bill, it will also force you to check the spending on that card more regularly, depending on your use patterns. That is, you'll be more likely to catch fraudulent charges sooner.

Where you park and the perils involved with that have already been discussed. Remember to park in well-lit areas. Stay away from spots that will box you in, like next to large trucks or SUVs. The cover concealment concept works for the bad guys too. Don't put yourself in a position where you might be walking into a trap of sorts. Do not leave valuables in plain view in your car, such as gifts, cell phones, purses, clothing, etc. Put these items in the trunk or cover them up with a dark blanket. Make sure that, when putting them in the trunk, you are aware of the people around you.

I don't like big shopping malls. I think they pose too much of a risk to my safety, and it's not like I'm supporting little mom and pop shops. Yeah, okay, I'm not giving business to the calendar kiosk guy or dude that will repair my cell phone screen, but it's not like your run-of-the-mill small business owner is going to be exchanging commerce in these large mega malls. If you're lucky, you may have a shoe repair guy at a mall or kitschy ceramics painting studio. Most of your shops at these large malls support big corporations. Instead of opening myself up to several liabilities by roaming malls, I do most of my consumer shopping online. Take from that what you will. Everything else I buy, I do my best to support members of my community and small businesses, which in my opinion also poses a smaller risk to my safety. If you're going to go to big shopping malls, try to do so in pairs or groups.

Most of this may seem like it's basic common sense, but if it were, the number of people being ripped off or suffering a violent encounter would not be as high as it is. Your basic concepts on Defensive Mentality and color code of awareness will include some of these ideas, but to specifically highlight them, here are some tips to follow.

Be alert and trust your sixth sense. It is easy to get distracted looking at your holiday list, texting, or answering calls. Remember to always stay focused on your surroundings while you are shopping. If something feels off, or someone looks unsafe, trust your gut and ask for help.

Shopping with young children presents a problem all in itself. It is better to shop without children, but I realize that is not an option all the time.

When traveling through or leaving a mall, there are things you need to keep in mind. Avoid target bags, which are rich and high-profile (e.g., big white Apple bags). Anything that says I have money or goods that are expensive makes you stand out like a Christmas goose to a would-be thief. When walking to your car, keep your pepper spray or other defensive weapon handy. Having your pepper spray in your hand with your finger over the activation button is not overkill. While moving through stores, and the mall in general, if you think you are being followed, don't leave a particular store or area; instead, try to get by more people. Again, anything that can make you bigger, louder, or different from your surroundings is a good thing, and that includes bringing other players into the equation.

When you are going to your car after exiting the mall, follow the basic safety concepts previously covered. Always carry your keys in your hand while walking to your car. Only unlock the driver's side door, unless you need to open all the doors—usually one click, not two. Having your keys in your hand will also help to ensure you get into your car that much quicker. If you have a panic button on your keys, be ready to press it until you are in your vehicle and safe. You can use a pen or pepper spray as a weapon if necessary.

Go directly to your car. If you carry a purse, make sure to keep your money in your front pocket. Women should try to utilize a purse that is designed to be carried across your body, similar to a messenger bag. For men carrying a wallet, be sure to keep it in your front pocket. Most slacks or jeans do not have buttons on the back pockets, and they are extremely easy for pickpockets to snatch wallets and phones from.

Always load children before groceries or packages. They should all be placed in the car and car seats first. Then tend to the loading of the car, proceed back to enter, lock all doors, and go on your way. Never leave a child in the shopping cart seat while unloading. They can easily be snatched out or pushed away by a criminal.

Don't store your bags or items in the back seat. Or if you do, remember to cover them with a dark blanket. Piles of shopping bags or big boxes containing consumer electronics are exactly what a criminal who is intent on smashing a window and taking off with the goods is looking for. This is especially important if you have more shopping stops. If you have a hatchback with one of those cargo covers, use it. Anything you can do to mask what you have going on in your car should be employed.

This is not a time to dilly dally. Once you are belted in, drive away. If you have a phone call to make, text to send, or email to field, do that at another location. Sitting in a parking lot or garage at a mall makes you a fish in a barrel. Go somewhere else that has not been potentially cased to handle any business you need to. If you're like most people, your car would pair with your phone. Just wait until you are out of the area and then make that hands-free phone call. Be aware of your surroundings, and always trust your instincts.

The holiday shopping season leaves you more vulnerable. Carjackers and those intent on mugging you know that people buy a lot of stuff in the time period between Black Friday and Boxing Day. These carjackers and criminals make their living off of holiday shoppers. Not only will the jackers get your car, they'll get your stuff too. Just remember, it's not only Black Friday for businesses; the criminals get to meet their bottom line in the same time frame. Don't help them achieve their financial independence.

It's almost impossible to live your life without shopping being a part of it. If you do it safely, with a plan, and avoid high profile areas and situations, you can have a successful shopping experience! Don't be a meal ticket for criminals.

CHAPTER
07
Travel Protection

Planning

When talking about travel safety, preparation is key. Before you even leave your home, there are a number of things you need to consider. You're going to be traveling, away from home, possibly for a long period of time. Things you need to do leading up to your trip are pack and prepare. You're not only going to be preparing for your trip, but also preparing to leave your home in a secure state.

There is a colloquialism that we're supposed to always leave a note. When I was a kid, the text message system I had was writing a note on a scrap piece of paper or envelope for my parents to know where I was going to be and for how long. That practice was embraced through the twentieth century until text messages and emails became a thing. In the movie 127 Hours, and in the book that it is based on, a hiker heads off without telling anyone where he was going. That hiker subsequently gets his arm pinned between two rocks, and what transpires thereafter is a story of both enduring survival and tragic consequences. If Ralston, the hiker, had left a note, people may have been able to render aid to him in a more conventional way and go looking for him. What does this mean here? Well, leave a note with your close friends and loved ones! Tell them your travel plans.

A lot can happen to you when you're on the road, traveling by plane somewhere, or commencing with domestic or foreign travel. Whoever is your trusted person, presumably the same person that you're going to ask to look after your home and affairs while you're gone, should know exactly what you are doing and for how long. Give that person a list. It does not have to be an epic and detailed itinerary of what you are doing, although that is not a bad idea, but at minimum where you are going and for how long. Items to include are: departure date, mode of transport, flight numbers, hotel and accommodation name and address, any special destinations or activities that could have more risk (Sky diving? Bungee Jumping? Zip-lining? An area known for high crime, etc.), date of return, return flight information, and even taxi or ride share information. A general outline so that, if they should not hear from you or you never return, your potential location might be identifiable.

While you're gone, the absolute best thing you can have is someone to look after your place. This is not just a matter of making sure a pipe does not burst or something happens to your home, but will also aid in making the house seem occupied. If you're going to be gone for many days, a week, or more, someone that is casing the area to rob may pick up that your natural patterns are disrupted. Watch Home Alone and see how Harry and Marv make note of the patterns of the illusion of an occupied home. Not all criminals are smash- and-grab idiots. Some do plan quite well.

Things your friend or family member can do for you while you're away could be getting your mail. Hey, we may all love our trusted neighborhood mail carrier. Maybe you have a great relationship with him or her, maybe you have no clue who they are. Should you be traveling around the holidays or other high mail volume time periods, the USPS may employ temporary delivery persons. These people are not vetted as well as your full-time employee. If you have mail piling up, they'll know, and if they've got criminal intent or conspirators, the fact that you are away from home makes you a target. Yes, you could leave a note for your mail carrier or have a "hold mail" notice put at your local post office, but this essentially does the same thing, letting people know you're not going to be home! You may have to rely on that if you have no one to help you at home. But if you do have a trusted person getting your mail, it removes the mail from the box, also removing potentially personally identifiable information, and gives the illusion that someone is home. Traffic in and out of the home.

Newspapers and circulars are another issue to deal with. Stop delivery of any newspaper subscriptions for the time you're going to be away, or again, better yet, have someone pick them up for you. Nothing says "no one is home" like a pile of newspapers or circulars in a driveway.

A few other things your trusted person can do is move your car from spot to spot in your driveway. If it's your neighbor that is looking after your place, have them park in your driveway every few days. They can also come at different times of the day, to keep things random. Granted, this may seem like a lot to ask of a friend or family member, but if they commit to helping you, it can save you from coming home from your dream Wally World Vacation to a ransacked house.

Hardening tips that should be paid attention to, as discussed in the home safety chapter, include the use of light timers and fake TVs. Leaving a light on outside and in the front entrance of your home does give a better appearance than a home that has no lights on for days on end, but this should be on a timer as well. If the light is on all the time it has the opposite effect. If you have an old school radio that can be hooked up to a timer, use it to have some noise at different times in your home. Just the presence of a doorbell cam can prevent you from being robbed.

What I do before I travel is take photos on my phone of all of my identification and credit cards, and I save them in a Dropbox or Cloud account that I can access from any computer in the world. If my wallet or ID becomes separated from me in a foreign land, I can ask for access to Dropbox, and I can print out copies of all of my pertinent information. Keeping a list of all the hotel names, addresses, and other locations of interest during your trip is also a good idea. Whatever itinerary or "note" you leave for your trusted person, take a printed copy of it with you and have copies on the cell phones of everyone in your travel party.

Every year, thousands of electronic devices are lost and never recovered at airports and in planes. Most never get identified. If you want a chance of ever getting your device back, here is a tip. Make the screen saver image on your mobile device your business card or contact info, preferably not your home address. If your device is found, just tapping on the home button will reveal your contact info.

Packing

What you pack and bring with you on your trip is going to depend on what kind of person you are and what you are doing. There are going to be many different devices and products I'll discuss through this chapter, but first I'll cover a few things to think about when packing for your big trip. If you're going camping, hiking, or some other "ing" activity, chances have it you already have the "be prepared" mentality. Your daily needs will need to be met by what you bring, in addition to any of those "oh shit" moments. What about everything else?

One thing to bring with you is a multi-tool. MacGyver made a great profession of being a problem solver by using the precursor to the multi-tool, his trusty Swiss Army knife. I'm not suggesting that you'll have to disarm bombs, but there are a number of times a multi-tool may pay off to have. Remember, if you're traveling by air, this item must be in your checked baggage! It's good practice to have one of these handy for what may come.

A friend of mine once used his multi-tool to cut a ring off a friend's jammed finger while on a sailboat trip in the British Virgin Islands. That would have been a costly situation if they were not able to remove the ring and had to seek medical attention. Point being, use your imagination on why something like this could be handy when you're traveling. Just be sure you know the laws of where you are going. Not every country in the world smiles upon people having knives! Don't become an international headline!

A spare battery pack for your mobile devices is a good thing to have. While you're out and about on whatever trip you are on, you may have to top off your battery. Keeping one in your travel day bag might be something you want to do, as well as a conventional charger.

If you're traveling to a foreign country, know what the voltage and cycle is of the power supplied. You also want to know what type of plug they use. Some European countries, such as Germany, use the "Shucko" plug. Others like the UK use the "Type G." We don't need to go crazy here on this subject, just look up what type of adapter you need and find out what kind of power is supplied at your destination. Most electrical devices you're going to be traveling with are going to be computers or mobile devices. Many of the transformers that they use to power them are multi-voltage and take different cycles, so just check the label. Keep in mind, if a country uses a voltage that is higher than the United States, regular "American" surge protectors won't work, they will fry!

When you're traveling, this is NOT the time to bring all of your fancy jewelry with you. It's a time to wear that $30 Casio watch so you can spend more time enjoying your vacation with your family and friends, and less time worrying about your possessions. I will, however, always travel with my Apple Watch. I like it for the alerts and the time zone functions, as well as using it for the maps. I do not have to look at my phone, which frees up both of my hands. There is a give and take to this situation, and I feel a smart watch is more of a useful tool than a liability. They are appealing though, just keep that in mind.

Other items to take along might include: a small first aid kit that has pillow packs of whatever over-the-counter medicines you may want in it. You don't need anything fancy, just some bandages, antibiotic ointment, etc. Any medications you need, make sure you bring extra with you. This is especially important if they are life sustaining, such as ones to treat people with a thyroid condition, blood pressure issues, or people like transplant patients that need immune suppressants. If you are delayed coming home or caught up in some sort of bigger disaster, you don't want the thing that kills you to be your failure to prepare. A flashlight is also a must. You're going to want to keep one with you, certainly in your hotel in the event of a power outage or other emergency. More items to bring along will be discussed through the chapter, when they come up in context.

A compact, push button flashlight is always a must when traveling.

CrimeProofBook.com

At your destination

Many crimes are committed while people are on vacation because most people think that, when they are on vacation, the criminals are also on vacation. But in fact, what exists is a subset of criminals that work within a niche—preying on tourists. Whether it's auto travel, air travel, cruise travel, foreign travel, etc., most crime to tourists is grossly underreported. This is because, let's face it, if you and your husband only have six days a year to fly to an island and relax, and someone steals your $300 tablet device, do you really want to spend the entire day in a police department filing reports and being embarrassed that you were scammed for that $300? Most people will not report either out of embarrassment, being lazy, or just writing it off as stupidity, and hoping that it won't happen to them again.

When you're traveling in strange areas, you need to remember to be ultra-cautious and aware of your surroundings at all times. There are so many scams that occur. First thing I do when I check into a room is slip that lock over the door, the secondary lock. The next thing I do is use one of those little round Band-Aids (that I don't know the use of) and block the peephole. There's a small device that can be purchased on Amazon.com for $30 that you can put over a peephole from outside a door, which is a reverse peephole viewer. I show students this when we do classes here. It was designed for SWAT teams to look into a door through a peephole before they breached the door. Anybody can purchase one. They're not regulated.

When you check into your room, always block the peephole with a round Band-Aid or sticky note.

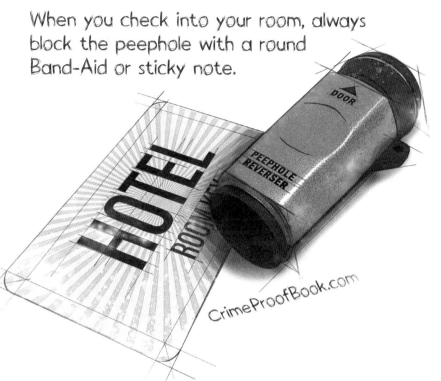

You could be sitting in your hotel room, counting money, and your computer could be laid out on a desk alongside your iPad, your iPhone, and all of your other devices. Someone is going to walk by, put that peephole viewer against the hole of the door—your peephole—and be able to see into your entire room. The first thing I do is lock the door; second thing I do is cover the peephole. The third thing I do is find the physical address of the hotel, if I don't already have it, I write it down on a post-it note, and I leave it next to the phone. I was in Orlando at the Shot Show about 10 years ago, and I got into a cab from the Florida Convention Center, and I said, "The Sheraton, please," and the cabdriver said, "Which one?" I said, "The one on International Drive." He said, "There's three on International Drive." So I thought about this. If I'm in my room at three in the morning and there's an emergency, I'm going to call 911, and I'm going to be telling the police "I'm on the ninth floor, room bla-bla-bla from the Sheraton." And I won't know which one I'm in. So, the physical address should be written and handy.

The next thing I do before I go to bed at night is take a bath towel and stick it under the crack of the door. This is there for three reasons: First, it cuts down on the noise that comes through the door from people walking around and talking throughout the night. The second thing it does is lessen my chances of asphyxiating from smoke should the hotel catch fire. And the third thing it does is prevent visitors in the middle of the night. What most people don't realize is, they think that gap under the door is cut real high so the hotel can slide that piece of paper bill through in the middle of the night on check-out day. That's one reason. The other reason is, they have a special tool in security called an Under the Door tool, or UTD. The UTD is slid under that crack of the door, turned 90 degrees, and it goes up and grabs the secondary lock, moving it off the door. All security departments have

tools like this in case someone barricades themselves into the room, passes out, gets hurt in the room, or dies in the room. They don't want to break the door and the door frame, so security has at least one of these tools under lock and key. There are other tools that might be employed that can slide between the door and the jam, pushing away swing bar locks, etc. While this is all technically for your "safety," it is also a security liability.

These devices also can be purchased readily on the open market. You think you're sleeping securely and someone can come right into your room at three in the morning. For me, they have to push through that towel. You can take it one step further; you can dampen that bath towel that you're going to put under the door. That will help to create a better airtight seal. Some people travel with a little 120-decibel piercing alarm that looks like a

120-decibel piercing travel alarm sets up in seconds.

CrimeProofBook.com

door wedge used to keep it open. They sell devices like that on the market. Also sold online are devices that hook to the doorknob so that, if it is turned, a 120-decibel alarm goes off. These are all viable options. But most people like to travel light, and they don't want to carry all this "extreme" equipment with them. If you feel you're in a dangerous area, you can always drag a piece of furniture in front of the door. But just remember, should there be a fire or emergency, and you have to exit in a fast manner, that might not be an option for you. Most of the crimes that occur to travelers are done as inside jobs by staffers of hotels, tourist companies, and security departments of respective companies.

Something I learned from a fireman to take note of; normally you shouldn't stay past the 11th floor at a hotel, because most fire ladders don't go past the eleventh floor. If you're staying on the twenty-sixth floor with a beautiful view, you have to hope you don't get trapped on that higher floor. I do break this rule from time to time. One rule I will try NOT to break is never staying on the ground floor of a hotel. It is too easy to break a window and come in. When I've been forced to stay on the ground floor in a motel, I keep the curtains drawn all the time. I do this because I don't want anybody to walk by and see whatever items or devices I have out on display for them to take note of and to come back and take from me when I'm not there.

Another thing to be aware of is, when you check into a hotel, the person at the desk should hand you your room keys with the room number written on the envelope. They should NOT say your room number out loud. If your room number is repeated out loud by the concierge or front desk, you should immediately demand a new room, and demand that they not say the number out loud. The way this scam works is, there's someone sitting in the hallway with a second person on the stairs of the hotel. They're going to radio up to each other what room you're in, and as you're walking into your room someone's going to burst in behind you, putting you at gunpoint or knifepoint and rob you. They can achieve all this because they know exactly what room you're going into and they've prepared to set you up. I always ask for two room keys, even if I am alone, and I always take a picture with my phone of the inside of the key holder where my room number is written so I do not forget what room I am in.

Another common scam is, you'll have a woman check into a room, or a male alone, the phone will ring, and it will be from a house phone that anybody can pick up in any waiting area of the hotel or any common area. They call your room and say, "Hi, this is George from Maintenance. We're having a problem with the hot water.

Can you check yours, please?" If the person answering the phone says something to their loved one like, "Go check the hot water," then the scam artist has a feeling there's at least two people in the room. But if a woman answers the phone and says, "Hold on, I'll check," and she goes and runs the water and comes back and says, "Ah, yes, the hot water is working." Then this George will say, "Thank you, ma'am. Someone from Maintenance might stop by to check the temperature of the water later. Just letting you know." Fifteen minutes later, knock on the door, the woman traveler looks through the peephole (hopefully she peels back the Band-Aid and looks through the peephole), and there's a gentleman with a uniform on, maybe wearing a hotel badge. What person would not open the door at that point? What you need to do at that point is say, "Hold on, sir," and then call the front desk and verify, in fact, that that person is a hotel employee. If your sixth sense tells you it does not feel right, you do not have to open the door for that person. You can tell them that they have to come back with a manager or security.

When ordering room service, always state that there is a minimum of two people that the service is for, even if you are alone, so that you do not transmit you are alone. If you are alone, shut the bathroom door when you let room service in so there is the element that there may be someone else in the room. Never leave a tag outside the door with a breakfast room service order that you filled out. A criminal can see this and set you up to gain access to your room pretending to deliver your breakfast.

If you bring valuables with you, be very wary of your in-room hotel safe. Many of these safes have a backdoor code programmed into them in case the last occupant forgot to leave it unlocked. I have found numerous times that four zeros will in fact open a safe that is locked. Of course, they also have an electronic device that hotel security uses to unlock the safe, which is also readily available to buy on the commercial market. I really never keep any valuables in that little safe. I keep my valuables with me, and many hotels will have a safe where you can store items when you're out and about from the hotel.

Out and about when traveling

Many threats will present themselves when you are actually vacationing while on vacation. People get preoccupied and distracted because, hey, you're supposed to be on leisure time. An unfamiliar area is not the place to let your guard down.

Something parents should do is, before they leave every morning to go out while on vacation, they should take a current picture of their child with the clothes they're in fact wearing that day, and have it backed up on their phone and other electronic devices (this advice is good for normal day-to-day life at home as well if going to malls or local theme parks). If they were separated from their child, they have THE most current picture to identify that child. There are child ID programs sponsored by different groups and they will make up a "kidnapping kit" for you. Many of them today include a dental impression, pictures, video, and fingerprints. In most of the kits, the media you are provided is digital, so you can take copies with you of all your child's information, fingerprints included, right on your phone.

Something else to work into your cache of safety items are dog tags. Not "woof woof" dog tags, but "GI Joe" dog tags. Truth be told, we could be talking "woof woof," but more on that later. There are many places online where you can snag metal embossed dog tags for cheap. You can find them for as low as five bucks a pair. If you're lucky, the vendor will also allow you to put different information on each tag in the pair. Why is this helpful? If you have toddlers or small children that are ultra-mobile, that may get away from you or easily lost in a crowd, you can give them their very own cool GI Joe dog tag.

The information on these tags should be limited to the parent's names and cell phone numbers. In the event you get separated, expect the worst, but hope for the best—the best being that a good Samaritan will help your child, see the dog tag and/or your kid may point it out to them, and then call you to bring you back together. The "woof woof" tags can be just as effective. These can be purchased from machines at the exits of many big box

stores or inside large pet stores. Put the same information on those tags and lace them on your child's sneakers a few rows of laces down.

Dog tags can also be used as luggage tags. Where you are is going to determine what type of luggage tag you use and what you put on them. Say you're headed for a family vacation to Wally World. You might want to make up extra dog tags with the same information you have on the ones for your children (name and number), and put them on things like camera bags, fanny packs, diaper bags, etc. Use heavy-duty zip ties or split rings to secure them to your stuff. Again, hope that, if you're separated from your items, someone that has good intentions will find them and try to notify you.

For luggage tags that you put on your suitcases and checked baggage, don't use your home address. Use your work address if possible. This way baggage handlers that are passing luggage along, or other prying eyes, won't take note of your address and then be able to use that information to rob you or sell the information to other thieves. Your destination and luggage size may be enough to tip people off about how long you're going away. Flying to France with several big suitcases? You're probably going to be gone for a while. Security luggage tags are also available that obscure most of your information unless someone takes them apart to see the whole tag.

There are a whole host of companies that make great bags that you can buy for traveling. One company is called PacSafe, which makes bags and clutches for men and women that have cable built into the straps so that it is very hard for someone to cut your bag off of your shoulder. Their product line also includes backpacks, camera bags, and other options. They also have wire mesh in the bottom of the bag to prevent someone with a razor from cutting the bottom of the bag open and spilling out your contents. A common scam in Europe, especially in Rome, is to have a pretty woman distract a man or a good-looking man distract a woman tourist, and someone will come to the other side and, with a razor, cut the bottom of your bag with their bag open-mouthed underneath it, so that all of your contents fall into it. Something you need to be aware of. The PacSafe company has excellent customer service and stands by their products. A friend of mine had some wear on the straps of one of his camera bag backpacks, and PacSafe sent him a brand new one to replace the damaged one.

You also have to be careful when you're leaving your hotel or leaving a restaurant to go back to the hotel that you are staying at. You need to ensure you are getting into a legitimate cab or ride share. Many people have been robbed and/or worse by getting in a vehicle that was not a real cab. When you're leaving the hotel, you should have hotel staff summon a legitimate cab for you. When you're leaving the restaurant, you should approach a cab and make sure that they have all of their licensing and credentials mounted on the dashboard. Again, this is a time where you need to rely on your sixth sense. If something doesn't feel right, there's a good chance it's not

Wire reinforced
straps

Lockdown point
for zippers

RFIsafe™
pockets

Hidden stainless
steel wire mesh

CrimeProofBook.com

right, and you don't want to make that decision AFTER
you're in someone's so-called cab, on your way to the joy
ride of your life.

When scheduling a ride, always share it with a friend or family member. All of the ride sharing apps have that option. All you need to do is press "Share Status."

This is also a good time to check the driver's rating as well. Confirm the vehicle, license plate, and the driver when they arrive. This is the time to stop whatever you are doing and focus. When riding alone, NEVER sit in the front seat! The most tactical spot is in the back seat opposite the driver. When you open the rear door of a ride share car or taxi, ALWAYS check that the little switch on the inside frame of the door is not clicked to the "child lock" position! This will prevent you from opening the door from the inside. As a matter of fact, if this switch is set for "lock," do not enter the vehicle at all! If it is, alert the driver to open the door and disable it. This is when it is handy to have a tactical pen with a glass breaker on it. Many newer model cars have the child lock switch that is controlled by the driver of the vehicle. I recommend that, as soon as you open the car door, before getting in, lower the window down entirely, then close the door and see if the door will open. I always keep the window slightly opened as well. The window is much easier to break if escape is needed when it is slightly open. Just grabbing the top of the window with your hands and pulling can break it to create an exit.

Never enter a ride share if you confirm the child safety lock is LOCKED!

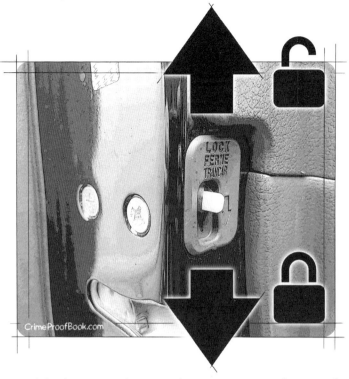

Track your ride to make sure you are being taken to the proper destination. I also recommend you talk with someone from your mobile phone the entire trip and give them status updates as you travel, loud enough for the driver to hear as well.

Another thing that is important to bring up is footwear. Let's face it, when we're on vacation, trying to relax and enjoy ourselves, we do try to leave everything behind. When you're scheduled to go on a trip to some all-inclusive resort, beach destination, or any other "warm weather" location, flip-flops and sandals are usually on your packing list. Regardless of where you are going or what you are doing, the proper footwear can make or break your experience. Make sure you have quality, broken in, sturdy, well-fitting footwear. While on vacation is not the time to break out a brand-new pair of sneakers, so make sure you zip around in them a bit to break them in before heading off into the unknown. This is of particular importance if your trip is going to include a lot of walking.

If you're sitting on a beach sipping margaritas, you're liable to have on the aforementioned flip-flops, etc. Flip-flops, sandals, crocs, water shoes, etc. are all liabilities in a shit-has-hit-the-fan scenario. All you need to do is think about something happening and you and your family need to run. Give this a test drive, put on some flip-flops and go for a jog. Visualize yourself in a Condition Red scenario and then having to flee from a fire, active shooter, bombing, mugging, or some other unplanned emergency. There are plenty of images of people in NYC the day of 9/11 running in suits and dress shoes. I'm confident running in dress shoes or high heels was not helpful to these people. If you're going to be letting your hair down in the footwear department, keep this in mind, and/or consider getting Tevas or other "active" leisure footwear that have real soles, support, and secure strapping.

This advice goes for "boat shoes" and moccasins too. If you're going for a trendy yuppie or yachtie casual-dress look, don't let your shoes hold you back. Get quality shoes that will stay on your feet! If that means sneakers, don't be afraid of looking out of style. You'll thank me if you're at a beach bar fleeing an active shooter scenario, with tables of raw oysters being flipped over and piña coladas going into orbit.

Airport and airplane safety

While traveling by air, you're essentially completely disarmed. Air travelers have very few options when it comes to defending themselves in an airport or on an airplane.

One thing you can have with you is a tactical pen. There are all different kinds of tactical pens on the market. You want to make sure your pen is not one of the ones that has a "DNA collector" tip or sharp end. Honestly, a standard ballpoint pen can be used for self-defense, if used properly. But, if you're looking for something with a bit more teeth, go tactical. If a tactical pen does not suit you, then look into some of the higher quality metal pens. The Cross Century line of pens is sturdy, good looking, write well, and will pack a serious punch if you need to use it as a striking item to defend yourself. A step up would be the thicker Cross Century Two line. There are a multitude of options in this category; you just need to seek them out. All of those pens you can get through security, provided there is nothing sharp or threatening looking about them. Note: If you carry a tactical pen that has a glass breaker tip, chances are TSA will confiscate it.

I will say, though, a buddy of mine travels with a tactical pen that does have a menacing point on the end. He's never had an issue with TSA when having one of those bad boys in his carry-on bag. The only place he was ever hassled was at Wally World, when a security guard who was originally from New York City, go figure, stopped him

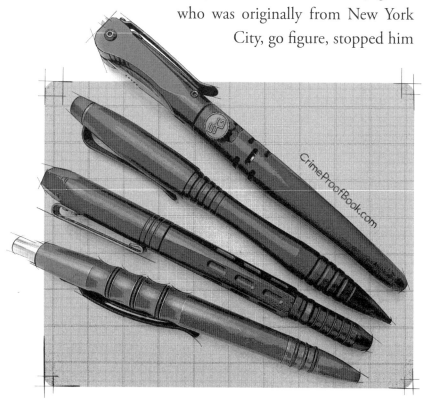

because he saw the clip on his pocket. The guard thought it was a knife and, after showing the astute New Yorker it was a pen, the guard recommended the clip not show, as it appeared to be a knife. Years of travel and many trips to theme parks, through airports, a courthouse, and high security locations, that was the one and only time he was stopped, hassled, or questioned about his pointy tactical pen. Take from that what you will. Just be willing to surrender anything you do have should it look threatening to any TSA agent.

Another improvised weapon you can put together, specifically when on an airplane, is a make-shift flail. I like to take with me in my carry-on bag a pair of those knee-high nylon socks. Make sure they are not too thin. What you can do is, when the flight attendant asks you what you want to drink, request a "can of diet cola, and please don't open it yet." Once you have your can of soda, you can leave it on your tray table next to your nylon socks. Should you need a weapon, slide the can of soda into the sock, and now you have a business casual flail of the 21st century! Think of the damage you can do if you swing one of those bad boys around, striking a hijacker in the head.

Someone I know travels with a fake Babe Ruth signed baseball in one of those acrylic protective cases. It looks like an important collectors' item, so suspicions are low when going through security. This is especially true if it's signed. No one is going to break out the Pawn Stars microscope to confirm it's the real deal! Then when he's on the plane he'll put his prized possession on the tray table next to the socks. Not only is it there to be an improvised weapon, it'll be a hell of a talking point should he get stuck next to one of those people that just want to talk the whole flight. Use some thought here. What else can you bring on a plane to use as the weighted end of your improvised flail?

If you are in a "routine" hijacking and the plane is headed to a new destination or being held for a ransom, it may be best to comply. If the hijacking looks like the plane is being turned into a bomb like we saw on 9/11, then a fight to the death must ensue!

When you are in an airport, get through TSA as quickly as possible. In fact, try to plan trips at off times so that TSA will be less crowded. The side of the airport after security is much safer from terrorist attacks and/or criminals. You also want to make sure you wear clothing that does not stand out; you want to blend in with everyone around you.

One thing you can do to expedite your wait time in the TSA line is enrolling in one of the Trusted Traveler Programs. The two most common are TSA Precheck and Global Entry (GOES). Sure, you have to pay a fee for these and show up in person to apply, but they pay off if you travel a lot. Once registered in one of these programs, when you make your airline reservations, make

My 2 favorite travel items.

sure you list your
known traveler ID number
where applicable. You should be issued a boarding pass that says "TSA Pre Check" on it. With such a boarding pass you get several perks. The line is usually shorter, although people are getting more on-board with the program, but there are other benefits. You won't have to remove any

electronics from your carry-on bag, take off any belts, take your shoes off, or remove light jackets. You plop your stuff on the belt and walk through a traditional metal detector. I also have enrolled in CLEAR; this is a retina ID-based system that adds more speed to me moving through the airline and safely past TSA.

While going through security, I like to keep all my important stuff in my PacSafe travel bag. Everything is organized and secure. Being organized and ready to go through the metal detector or millimeter wave machine will keep your exchange somewhat painless. Something else you can do to make security a breeze is wear a nylon belt with plastic buckle. Jump on the internet and look for wide, all nylon gun belts. They are sturdy and last a long time. These won't set off metal detectors, and that is the key benefit.

Going back to medications that you are required or may want to take, make sure you keep all of that in your carry-on bag. Should you get separated from your checked bag, which does happen even with the tracking systems they have, you'll have any important medications. Again, you don't want to die because you failed to have life-sustaining medication with you if you get separated from them.

You should do the same when you leave an airport, get out as soon as possible. There is no reason to linger.

Always try to schedule non-stop flights to minimize time spent in terminals.

Your luggage, however, needs to be discussed too. I hate black luggage! Have you ever noticed that ninety percent of the luggage at the baggage return is black? My luggage is bright red, very easy to spot, and much harder to steal. When you arrive at a destination, get your baggage and leave the airport as quickly as possible.

Look into the January 6, 2017 Fort Lauderdale airport shooting that occurred at the baggage terminal. I'll be talking more about active shooter events in another chapter, but that particular event needs to be mentioned as a prime example for you to not hang around. Always scan your surroundings whenever you are in an airport, looking for abandoned briefcases, packages, or suspicious items. Anything suspicious should be reported to airport authorities. Then leave immediately.

Elevator safety

This section could be in the safety outside of your home chapter, as elevators are in several locations that you may encounter in your daily life. If you work in a high-rise, this information could be pertinent in the safety at work chapter. Since most people when they are traveling and staying at hotels will encounter elevators, it is here. Regardless, this subject has its ups and downs—get it?

Elevators for criminals are like fishing in a barrel. Sexual assaults, robberies, and muggings happen all too often in elevators. When entering an elevator, look up into the back corners of the car and see if there are any mirrors set up. These are installed for security purposes so that you can see if someone is hiding on the left or right behind the doors. If someone is there, back away to safety. If the doors open and the occupants make you feel uncomfortable, do not get in. Back away and wait. If you are waiting for an elevator and someone approaches to also get in with you and you have a bad feeling, trust your senses and do not get in with that person. If someone gets on the elevator right after you stepped in and you have that feeling, press the next floor button and get off.

When I am in an elevator I "own" the buttons, and you should, too. I always stand next to the buttons with my back to the wall looking at the doors. When someone enters, I ask, "what floor?" and I press the buttons. This also keeps me in control of the alarm button as well.

If you are assaulted in an elevator, you must fight, make as much noise as possible, get to the buttons, and press the alarm. Try not to ever let anyone be behind you in an elevator. They can easily ambush you. Hug that wall whenever possible.

If you are carrying a purse, remember to keep it close to your body. Thieves and pickpockets work in teams as well, and one will distract you while another robs you. This is an excellent time to be trained in defensive pen or Kubotan when a firearm may not be a defensive option.

Train security

If you are traveling by train, travel in the guard's compartment if possible. These guard cars are identified by a blue light. If you can't be in a guard's compartment, find a carriage that has groups of people who could assist if needed and be good witnesses. Travel in groups of friends whenever possible. Try to arrive at the station as close to the departure time of the train as possible, and stand where the station is well lit. Always try to sit in a tactical position like the ends of the train, where you have two walls behind you. Stay alert and aware the entire trip. When you are waiting for a train, stay as far back from the tracks as possible, with a wall or column behind you until the train arrives.

I hope that you found these travel safety and security concepts to be helpful. As you can see, preparations are imperative when embarking on an extended journey away from home. If you don't employ all these tips—and not all of them will work for everyone—at minimum contemplate them and their possible implications/substitutes to keep you and your loved ones safe and secure.

CHAPTER
08

Campus Protection

I wanted to add this chapter on campus protection because your children are, in fact, your most valuable assets. Many children go off to college and they'll either stay on campus or off campus. Parents are extremely protective and overprotective of their children, and once they go to a campus, they lose that control. And for many parents, out of sight is out of mind. Hope that you have instilled the proper mentality into them, and be full of faith that they will make good decisions because of your influence.

When you bring your child to that campus and you're setting them up in the dorm room, as a parent you should look around and make sure that all of the hallways and the fire exits are well marked. Check that security is, in fact, being used in the building. When you go to your child's dorm room, there are some items in there that you might want to add to your list. Most people will make sure that their children have the little refrigerator, the newest iPhone, and the best laptop. However, parents won't spend a few hundred dollars to buy them a fire extinguisher or a ladder to throw out the window, should they be caught in a fire on the second or third floor. How about a personal alarm that can go on the doorknob that they can set before they go to bed at night? These are items that we should also be thinking about. There's nothing wrong with buying your child a plug-in smoke and carbon monoxide detector to keep plugged in in their dorm room either. I'm a suspenders-and-a-belt type of person, and these are more devices that could be used to protect them.

How about setting up a small bag of essentials for your child in case of an emergency, aka a "bug out bag"? This bag could have light sticks, some MREs (these are prepacked portions of food that usually just need a heat source and water. Some can be eaten at room temperature as well), some packets of water, and other non-perishable items. You could put some other survival tools in it, like a knife

or a flashlight, or maybe a Red Cross emergency radio. You can literally spend $200 and buy a bag and outfit it with these items and then some. While you're at it, spend $400 and buy two bags. Tell your child to keep

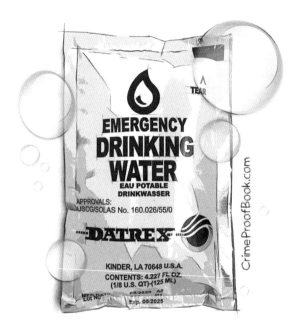

one in their vehicle if they have a car on campus, and another in their dorm room. To me, this is money better spent than a lamp, an end table, or a new pair of shoes for your most valuable asset.

The other thing you should do is check the local laws where your child is going to school. If appropriate, make sure they have mace or pepper spray. I feel pepper spray is a great option for security and defense. It's very important that your child is trained on the use of force and how to deploy mace, but it is more important that the mace is kept accessible to them at all times should they have to use it. How many times could a date rape have been prevented if the female student had deployed mace in that situation? At Gun For Hire, we teach self-defense mace/pepper spray use. We start as young as 13 years old and as old as 100,

As young as 13 years old can be properly trained.

and we've had numerous saves from people who have taken our class.

Another protection tool is a pen. A simple pen that you carry, a Bic pen or a Pentel pen, can be used for self-defense. At Gun For Hire Academy, we have a Defensive Pen class. Tactical pens are also an option, as mentioned previously. There are many pressure points and striking points that you can use as a force multiplier to get someone to comply. A great thing about a pen is it can be carried everywhere, and it's not frowned upon like a conventional weapon would be. This is something that is imperative to teach your children on how to use a device like a pen or a Kuboton for striking or putting someone into submission.

Another thing concerning campus security; you need to teach your child, especially females, that when they're out and about, someone

should always know where they are at all times (that 21st century note on an envelope to leave, aka text message or email at minimum). They should never drink

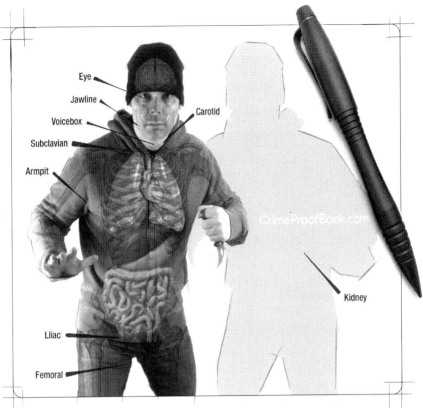

Eye
Jawline
Voicebox
Subclavian
Armpit
Carotid
Kidney
Lliac
Femoral

CrimeProofBook.com

Striking points my students learn in our protective pen class.

from a drink that they did not open, or watch get opened. Further, they should never drink any beverage that they left alone while they went to the restroom, etc. Instill that they should never drink any drink that they did not physically see being poured or did not pour themselves. Date rape drugs and "roofies" are out there in full force, and your child needs to be aware of this. In short, have them own the chain of custody of anything they are going to consume, knowing that it has not been tampered with. These simple safety techniques, which are not intrusive at all, can go a long way to protecting your child when you can't be there to protect them.

CHAPTER
09
Workplace Security

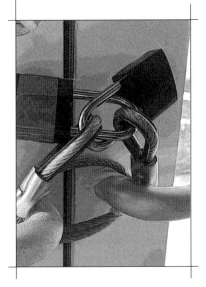

We spend a lot of time at our places of employment, and workplace violence needs to be taken very seriously. There are many instances of violence and stalking at work. There's an old joke about two people going on a long romantic walk but only one knows about it. It's not a laughing matter. People really need to take this into account.

Someone could be unhappy at their job, be terminated from the company, and maybe they will come back and start shooting people. You need to have the mindset that something can happen, or else you will fall into Condition White. And it's not hard for this to happen. You know everyone at work by their first name, you eat lunch with them every day, and you start to trust them. But if something doesn't feel right, it could be that it's not right. You could have a co-worker that shows no signs of anything being wrong, making it easy for you to just let it go when that person says or does something a little off.

Often, people will continue to let bad behavior slide because they don't want to be the person to bring something up to management. Inappropriate behavior should be reported to management, monitored, and documented. Always. Don't worry about rocking the boat, that is an antiquated idea.

I once worked for a defense contractor. While I was there, I had to give an employee a written warning. The next day, he took a picture of me. I asked what it was for, and he said target practice. He was fired and removed from the building, but for the next few months I was constantly looking over my shoulder. This is the kind of behavior I'm talking about. This is the kind of behavior that needs to be reported to the authorities.

I've talked about visualization and mindset, and work is a place where you need to use these skills as well. Think about this: Is my back to the wall? Many people work in a cubicle where their back is exposed. Try to change this if you can. Or you can try putting a rearview mirror on your computer. If you're in a position that is hard to defend, hang a mirror up so you can see who is coming up behind you. When you work with your back exposed, you probably shouldn't be working with headphones on. If you do, only use one or keep them soft.

You should also consider having mace in your desk drawer. You just have to keep in mind that sometimes kids

A computer mirror can give you the critical seconds needed to react.

come into your office and they could open the drawer. Also, your phone should be on you at all times in case you have to dial 911.

Let's say an active shooter came into your office. What would you do to respond? Where would you go and hide or shelter in place? Where are the emergency exits? You should have an emergency drill at work, at minimum in your mind. Look at your surroundings. What defensive tools do you have? Can you go into a room that has an egress window or door?

If your door locks, make sure the lock works. Buy door stoppers and keep them in the supply room. Put panic buttons in key locations around your workplace and have a few on keychains that people carry with them. We have 12 of them here at the range.

You also have to be careful about workplace theft. Don't ever leave your purse, personal belongings, or personal information in plain sight. Lock your purse or other belongs in your desk if you have to get up from your area, even if it's just for a minute. It's not just your co-workers who you need to be suspicious of. Cleaning companies can come in at night and rob from you.

Don't ever leave spare house keys around your office or anything with your personal address on your desk. All of these things open you up to becoming a victim of crime. Remember, predators look for easy prey.

Never EVER be alone at your workplace. That's a prime time for sexual assault to happen. You should never be the only one to leave at night. Always tell a co-worker you are leaving. It's much better to walk out with someone. Beyond the criminal elements here, you don't want to be at work alone and end up having some sort of a medical emergency or occupational accident. If you are in the building alone, lock the exterior doors and set the perimeter alarm if possible.

Think about this if you are leaving alone: You could set the alarm, walk out of the office, turn the key, and someone can run up behind you, put a knife to your throat, and make you open the door back up. This is especially true if you work in any kind of medical office. Criminals think that doctors' offices may have painkillers, a prime reason why they'd be looking to get in. Don't ever let your guard down. Any type of business is susceptible to theft, but some have more risk than others. Businesses that deal heavily in cash are prime targets, so keep that in mind.

Offices do get broken into in the middle of the night. If you walk into your office in the morning and the lights aren't working, don't keep walking in. If you see something knocked over or out of place, don't walk in. Walk out and get help. Don't just assume everything is okay. If you walk in, you could walk into the middle of a crime scene or a crime in progress. Many people are reluctant to call the police because they don't want to feel stupid. They may even have a bit of normalcy bias going on. But it's better to err on the side of caution. The average

American hardly ever calls the police, but they are there to help us when needed.

Cameras are absolutely crucial in the workplace. They are so inexpensive to buy now, and they have storage in the cloud. If you're part of the decision-making process at your work, make sure you don't buy a crappy camera system from a big box store. You can definitely tell the difference. Think about times when you've seen news reports asking if you've seen this person. The ones with good cameras show a much clearer picture of the perpetrator. How laughable are the grey people that look like they are between 150 and 275 pounds, kinda male, maybe female, with grey skin, wearing a grey hoodie? Get outta here! Go quality! If there are no cameras at your workplace, you can scare lazy criminals off by having signs around your building warning people that they are being recorded, or put up fake ones.

When you are interviewing for a job, look around and see if the place looks safe. When you're working at your job, ask your superiors what the security plan is. Make sure they have an emergency plan in place. Everywhere I've worked I've had one.

Here's an example. Let's say you work in a factory setting. Illegally, many business owners will chain doors closed in factories. The owner or manager is concerned about the bottom line, and we've all heard the expression "inventory slipped out the back door." The locks are in place to keep less-than-honest employees from stealing. But what happens if there's a fire or other emergency,

you're trying to escape, and the doors are locked? If you see chained or locked emergency exits, notify the police or fire department immediately.

Look at doctors' and dentists' offices. They often have receptionists behind security glass, and the receptionist will have to buzz people in. That's very often done for their safety.

You have the right to feel safe where you work. It's okay to bring these issues up. It's not a joke. But there will always be a few people that don't care and a few that are hypersensitive. Then you'll have to go into Condition Orange at work because you don't know what another employee might do.

It is the job of the business owner to keep you safe. They should do everything in their power to keep their employees safe, and if something bad happens, it is their responsibility to get the police involved. They need to file a complaint on your behalf. If the situation continues to ramp up, then the next step has to be taken with the authorities. If you have a problem, you go to your employer, and get no help, the employer can be held personally liable. If the police get involved, they might run a report on the person you complain about, and they will alert management if there are other incidents in that person's past, and now management MUST take action to protect you and other employees as well.

If something happens and your employer won't go to the police, then you have to do it yourself. If you can't get the restitution that you want from your employer, then you have to find another job. You have to worry about your personal safety and the security of your family.

As discussed earlier, restrooms have their own hazards associated with them, especially if they are shared among multiple businesses in a large complex or building. Be extra vigilant in that situation. You may feel comfortable at work, but that is not the place to be in Condition White.

A very vulnerable area at many office complexes would be parking garages, decks, or lots. We've already covered security in parking areas in two other sections; however, I want to expand a little on it in the context of the workplace. Remember to try to head to your car and leave work in pairs. If you're expecting to be working late, go to the garage or lot during the day and try to move your car closer to the exit you'll be using. Should you not have someone to walk out to the car with, get a security guard, if you have them, to escort you to your vehicle. Remember to have whatever defensive weapons you may need in one hand (pepper spray, a tactical pen, etc.), and your keys in the other ready to hit the panic alarm if needed. When you're in a parking area, use any defensive tools to your advantage.

Work is work. That can be bad enough, or perhaps not. The fact is, as individuals, I'm sure there are things you'd rather be doing with your time than working. In reality, you may spend more time with your co-workers than you do with your own family, at least time when you're awake and not run down! Keeping in mind that your workplace is susceptible to all the same perils you'd have at home or while out and about is integral to keeping yourself safe! After all, what use would you be to your family if you were severely injured or worse while at work?

CHAPTER
10

Non-Lethal Weapons, Improvised Weapons, and Defense Techniques

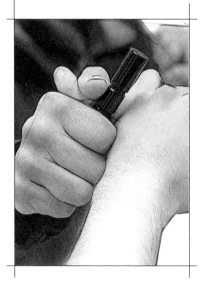

Where you live, are traveling to, or are located will dictate what you have available to you for self-defense. Beyond any statutory or legal hurdles to one's ability to defend themselves, there are moral implications. A question you need to be able to answer is, to what ends are you willing to go to defend yourself and/or your family? If the answer to the questions "is this weapon legal?" and "are you willing to use deadly force?" is "no," in one manner or another, then this chapter is for you.

To distill everything into two neat categories like that is not exactly fair, though. Something called "force escalation" needs to be considered. The basic concept is that force is to be met with like force. For example, if someone shoved you and you shot them as a defense, there is quite possibly an issue with how you escalated your use of force. The context to this is what is "reasonable," and what is "reasonable" to one person or another can vary in a big way. So, regardless of law and moral implications, you need to have options.

The legal and moral aspects of force escalation are beyond the scope of this book, but talking about the concept is important, as it is something that you're going to have to think about regarding your Defensive Mindset. I strongly recommend further training and education on this subject.

Non-lethal/less than lethal weapons

We're not going to spend a great deal of time on defining this. To keep it simple, we'll say that the weapon, whatever it is, does not have the potential to kill someone. Which is not exactly fair, as almost any object or weapon could kill someone, depending on how it's applied.

Many of the options available have been talked about throughout this book already. Well, here it all is in one nice, neat chapter. Discussing what is reasonable in different scenarios is an important process to instill your own idea generation. Some of these weapons can cross over between non/less lethal and improvised. Your less lethal options can include:

Aerosol self-defense spray:
Products and product categories included in the family of aerosol self-defense spray would be anything someone would spray in the face of an attacker to stop them. The trademarked product name Mace is one such product. Mace was specifically diluted from tear gas. Mace the product became Mace the company and now offers defensive spray in the form of pepper spray, aka oleoresin capsicum spray (OC spray), abandoning their original chemicals due to concerns of toxicity. All this means is that people may use the term Mace, pepper spray, and OC spray synonymously. Bear in mind, Mace is a trademarked name or a type of pepper spray. We're talking champagne verses sparkling wine here, folks. The importance of pepper spray is that, when sprayed into the face and eyes of an attacker, it will temporarily blind and stun them. The strategy would be to flee to safety while an attacker is out of commission.

Kubotan:

With the Kubotan, we're going to run into the same kind of sparkling wine/champagne situation as we did with OC spray. Kubotan is a trademarked name for a self-

defense keychain. Originally, the Kubotan got its name from Takayuki Kubotan, who developed them for police officers. They are fashioned after a small bamboo stick weapon, five to six inches long, made of various hard materials, and are used as a striking weapon or a tool to invoke submission by applying to pressure points, etc. There are different types of defensive keychains and spikes available. The Kubotan is a modern Yawara stick, and its simplicity makes it so effective that an individual would not need any special training for rudimentary use.

Tactical pen:

Tactical pens and/or regular ballpoint pens can be used in the same manner as a Kubotan. There are a host of different styles, some fashioned after Kubotans, some sleek and smooth with tapered lines, and others with castellated parapet tops which will inflict maximum damage while collecting a little DNA in the process (chunks of skin and hair). Most tactical pens are low profile and can be brought anywhere a plain pen can go.

Electronic/electro shock weapons:

Tasers and stun guns are weapons that fall into the electronic weapon category. These are considered less than lethal; however, people have been killed by having one of these deployed on them. Taser is a trademarked name for an electronic weapon. There are two different types of electronic weapons, one that has the electrodes on the body of the unit and one that will deploy the electrodes and be able to be shot from a distance. In general, stun guns refer to units where the electrodes are stationary and a user must be in close proximity of their threat to use it.

Improvised weapons

The subject of improvised weapons can go on ad nauseum. Almost anything can be used as a weapon. This is why the term "assault rifle" is not only a misnomer, it's a misnomer of laughable proportions. If I hit you with a hammer, does that make it an "assault hammer"? Improvised weapons in this context will fall into two categories, planned and unplanned.

Your planned improvised weapon will include the dress-casual flail we discussed in the travel chapter. The one where you would slide a full soda can, baseball, or other weight into a nylon sock to use as a striking weapon. A tactical pen could be considered an improvised weapon, as it is a pen.

The key to improvised weapon use is that you have a perfectly good explanation for having the item, and your intent to have the item is for its intended purpose. Walking around with a ball-peen hammer hanging from a loop on your belt, in the event you need it to bludgeon an attacker, would probably not be looked at as an improvised weapon. However, if you were a carpenter that was being violently attacked and knocked down, having your head beat into the concrete, and you grab a hammer out of your hammer loop because you're on the job, for defense, that may be looked at as self-defense using an improvised weapon. I talked about this concept in the section about keeping a Maglite in your car as a defensive weapon. This is all about optics!

This conversation is very important to have. In New Jersey, where the right to self-defense is extremely limited and unlawful possession of a weapon charges could include having a slingshot, a very peculiar criminal court case was decided in 1990. In State v. Kelly, the defendant was reported for being harassed by an ex domestic partner. Her former partner, Randolph Boone, had issued a number of threats to her safety. The particulars of the case involve Kelly arming herself with a box cutter, in the event she needed to defend herself from Boone. As luck would have it, Kelly did, in fact, end up using the box cutter in a self-defense situation. She ended up having three charges levied against her: aggravated assault, possession of a weapon for an unlawful purpose, and possession of a weapon "under circumstance not manifestly appropriate for such lawful uses as it may have."

The aggravated assault charge and possession of a weapon for an unlawful purpose charge were both dropped. The possession of a weapon for an unlawful purpose, and possession of a weapon "under circumstance not manifestly appropriate for such lawful uses as it may have" charge ended up ultimately sticking. Due to the nature of New Jersey's law, a box cutter is not intended to be used as a weapon. Since she admitted (more on that later) to police that she, in fact, carried the box cutter for the purpose of defending herself, a use "not manifestly appropriate," she implicated herself, and thus the charge was upheld by the jury. There are many lessons to be learned about this case. One is do not volunteer any information to the police without an attorney present, which will be expanded on further. And two, had Kelly found the box cutter, or any other weapon, while the attack was happening, the case would have been looked at through a different lens. Granted, the case and situation have more depth to them; however, it points out the perils of improvised weapons and the optics attached to them.

Given that, if you're going to be using an improvised weapon, you better happen upon it at the time of the attack or have a damned good reason as to why it was in your possession in the first place. This is of particular importance in jurisdictions where the laws of self-defense vilify victims that attempt to protect themselves.

Defense techniques

Should a weapon of any kind not be an option, you are left with your bare hands and, of course, whatever you can scrounge up, as discussed previously. There are defensive techniques that you should be aware of. Most of this is common sense; however, I would not be doing my job if I did not at least bring this up. When a violent encounter occurs and you do not have a force multiplier, the situation is "no holds barred!"

If you get physically attacked, fight like your life depends on it, because it does. Stick a finger in the attacker's eye socket, kick them in the groin, rake your fingers over them. Do anything you can to hurt them, even if it's temporary. You can bite the person with the force of a pit bull. Jam your keys into their face. Fight dirty! Directing your attack towards the eyes, ears, groin, and nose will have the biggest effect. Your loved ones, I imagine, would not be very judgmental if you told them you bit off someone's ear if they were trying to rape you. If anything, you'd get a bit of street cred. You want to make sure that you are the one that survives.

There's a period of time after which criminals will say, "That's it, people will see me, I gotta go." It's usually about 10 to 15 seconds and then it will dawn on the criminal, "Oh crap, I picked the wrong person,

I gotta get out of here." Yelling "fire" while employing defensive techniques will also make you bigger, louder, and different than your surroundings. Again, why "fire?" Because fire attracts everyone's attention. Make the perpetrator want to retreat.

Solar Plexus: Hub for nerves, arteries, and organs.

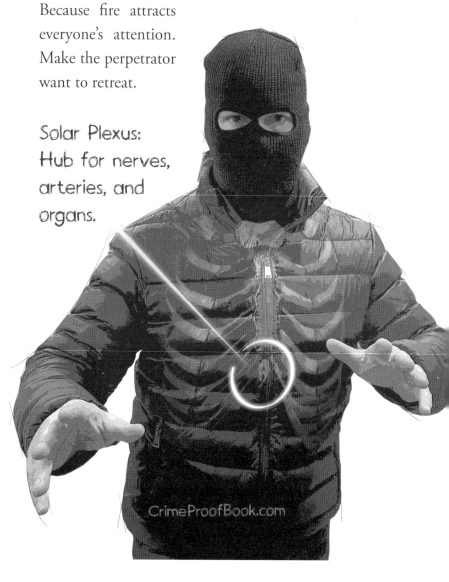

CrimeProofBook.com

There are certain levels of training. You can roll up a magazine and strike someone in the solar plexus as an improvised weapon (the solar plexus is a bundle of nerves in the center of the abdomen just below the chest). You can get training in martial arts or some other self-defense training. None of these are bad ideas. Your life does depend on it. I'd rather see you escape with scratches or scars and get out alive.

Last thing to remember. If you get accosted in any location, never let the attacker take you to a secondary location. Don't go with them if they say, "Come with me, and I won't hurt

CrimeProofBook.com

you." Your chances of survival are better if you don't go to a secondary location. Fight like hell, and hopefully you'll be able to live to talk about it.

CHAPTER
11
Firearms

Is a firearm for you? Some ins and outs to consider

The very first thing you need to do when you're considering a firearm for self-defense is decide if this is a viable option for you. Think about your religious and moral beliefs. Would you be able to handle possibly taking the life of another human? You can't recall a bullet once you've fired it. This is a huge decision that you are putting on yourself and your loved ones. It should not be taken lightly. Guns are not for everyone. You could end up shooting the wrong person. Could you live with that? Think long and hard about it before you make the decision.

Another issue is what happens if you live with someone else, you want a gun, and they don't? Your decision can have an effect on your relationships. If an accident happens, you may have to deal with "I told you so" for the rest of your life.

If you decide to get a firearm for self-defense, you can't just get a gun and some ammunition and stick it in the nightstand. That's just the tip of the iceberg. There's a lot more to it than that. You need guidance and training on purchasing the right gun for you, and you must learn how to use it. Never just rely on the salesman in the gun store. Most of the time they are there to make the sale. They will spend five minutes with you telling you how to put the bullets in the gun and send you on your merry way.

If you decide to buy a gun, you'll need to research what type you want (see more on that in the next chapter). Go through the NRA. Find an NRA course in your area, sign up for it, take the basic course, and learn from experts. You'll get a variety of guns to fire and plenty of range time. Think about your needs and your physical capabilities. Do all of that before you buy a gun. Knowing how to shoot a gun is going to help you select one!

You'll also have to think about accessibility and storage for your gun. You shouldn't go cheap on storage options. Can you safely store it? Will it be accessible when you need it? Too many people say, "I'm gonna get a gun in case something happens," and have no idea what to do with it. In an upcoming chapter, we'll explore gun storage a bit more.

You need to look into the laws in your state. You'll need to know about your homeowners' insurance. Does it cover you if you shoot someone in your home? Can you get an umbrella policy for that purpose? Do you have legal representation that you can call in the middle of the night if you need them?

If you decide that a gun isn't for you, there are other layers of protection for you in your home, including lights, alarms, mace, and cameras. A gun is not for everyone. If it's not for you, read on for the other preparedness tips in this book.

Range etiquette

If you do decide to bring a firearm into your toolbox of self-defense options, practicing with it is going to be important. After getting good training, developing and working on those skills should be done. Those skills are perishable, and you should schedule periodic trips to the range. At a minimum, I recommend going at least once a month. Granted, I understand that things get in

CrimeProofBook.com

This Gun For Hire challenge coin features the 3 important safety rules. This is handed to every young shooter.
1. Keep gun pointed in a safe direction.
2. Keep your finger off the trigger until ready to shoot.
3. Keep gun unloaded until ready to use.

the way and that it's not so easy with today's demands, but this is a goal you should try to meet. You don't have to go for an all-day range session, but shooting one box of ammunition during a quality practice session will do the trick. You'll have to go to a range to do this, and we need to cover that.

I am not going to go over the entire list of range rules and regulations in infinite detail. I just want to share some of my almost 40 years of experience in public and private ranges. ALL ranges have different rules and regulations, and all ranges have a different vibe towards newbies. When you arrive at a range, introduce yourself to the Range Safety Officer (RSO) and let him/her know if this is your first visit to the range. The RSO will tell you what you need to know before you set up your gear. Make sure you read the rules, regulations, and what ammo is allowed or not. It is always better to ask than assume.

Concerning the range rules and policies of a particular facility, you can always go online and see if they have them posted. If they do, then you have a chance to review them in advance, saving some time when you get there and allowing you to come prepared with questions. Not all facilities will have this online for a multitude of reasons, but some do.

I have seen people thrown out of ranges for intentionally shooting the target posts or the metal clips holding the target. Don't be that person. Learn the rules, follow the rules, get to know the staff, and be receptive to learning and taking input from the employees. Learn their names—that goes a long way—and remember to thank them after you clean up and before you leave. If you follow my advice, you will find yourself in the "in" crowd more often than not. There is a lot of knowledge in a gun store/range, and if you show a willingness to learn, there are many who are ready to teach.

Always remember, when in the range port, keep your finger off the trigger until you are ready to discharge the firearm, always point the firearm down range, and never turn around with the firearm in your hands.

You should always be aware of your surroundings while at a range, and in particular there are the new inexperienced shooters that you have to focus on as well as the "experienced" shooters that know it all. The latter tend to have the most safety issues at a range.

CHAPTER
12
Selecting the Best Gun and Ammunition

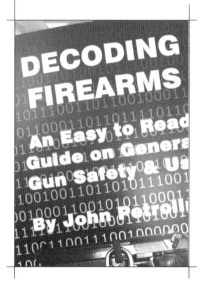

What's the best gun for you? There is no black and white answer to this question. It depends on your physical limitations, needs, budget, and your state and local laws. I have always felt that the best home defense firearm is a handgun. You can wield it with one hand and be on your phone with the other hand. Pistols are not cumbersome to move with or handle.

I tend to like revolvers, but they have limitations on ammunition capacity. In New Jersey, for example, you're limited to ten rounds of ammunition in a semiautomatic, which is still more than the standard six that most revolvers hold.

The best way to decide is to seek out a professional and try a few guns. There is help. You can use the NRA or consider getting a book called *Decoding Firearms* by John Petrolino, which is a soup-to-nuts primer for gun owners, new ones in particular.

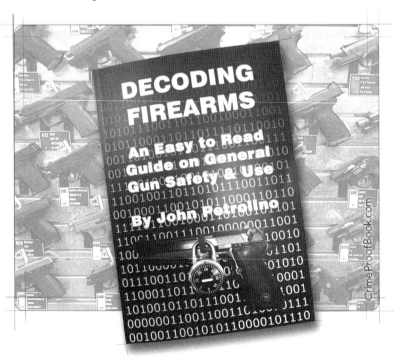

After you've made a decision on what type of gun you want, whether it be a long gun, pistol, revolver, semiautomatic, etc., you have to think about your budget and the make and model you want. If you live in an anti-gun state, you should be cautious as to what you buy. If you shoot someone with a seven-or eight-inch barrel 44 magnum, you could have prosecutor saying in court that you are a "Dirty Harry" wannabe. If you want a court-proof gun, buy one that is widely accepted by police or military. For example, a 10mm could be considered "extra deadly." A Glock 19 or 17, which 80 percent of law enforcement carries, is court-proof. Better yet, call your local police department and ask what service firearm and ammunition they use.

Make sure you don't buy too much or too little gun. For an average person with no disabilities, a 9mm or .38 caliber revolver would be the right way to go. Other guns will be construed as excessive by law enforcement. But too small of a gun will not have the stopping power that you may need.

Buying a gun is a game of weighing what works for each individual person. At my range, we pair guns to owners all the time. For example, women may have less upper body strength and smaller hands, generally, than men, so their needs are different. People's needs change as they get older. People can develop arthritis or carpal tunnel syndrome, which makes their gun needs different. A person's ability to manipulate a firearm can change if they lose strength or dexterity.

The fastest growing segment of gun owners is females. Gun ownership used to be an old boy network, but it's not like that anymore. Most guns that you can purchase now are unisex.

After you've purchased your gun, the next thing to think about is ammunition. You need something that reliably fires through the gun you've chosen but is widely used by police or military. There's something out there called Zombie Max ammo. It literally has pictures of zombies all over the box. If you were to use that for self-defense, you could find yourself in trouble with prosecutors. The picture they paint would be that you are a paranoid believer in zombies. Don't be that person.

Hollow point ammunition is safer than round nose bullets. Hollow point bullets expand upon impact. For home defense, use hollow point bullets. Make sure you check the laws where you live or will be with your firearm, though, as hollow point ammunition may be regulated heavily or prohibited.

You've now got your gun and ammunition. The next thing you need to do is make sure you shoot the gun you're going to be using for self-defense in practice sessions. You need to know that it will work when you need it. As noted earlier, going to the range at least once a month is recommended.

What about accessories? I'm not a huge advocate of lasers, red dot sights, or flashlights on guns. Anything with batteries I don't like. Most shootings happen seven feet or less away from the target, and the average shots fired is at three. You don't need scopes or anything else. You really should stick to the basic fundamentals, that way there's less to break, fewer batteries to die, and less crap to deal with when things go wrong. Remember the physiological changes you will go through in the course of an adrenaline dump during an escalated force situation and what that may mean concerning the gear you select.

How much should you pay for a gun? A ballpark figure for a gun is $500 to $800 as an average. You can spend up to $5000. You can buy used guns too, but I recommend a new one for a new owner. You'll also need to think about how many you need. You may need more than one!

Some houses need a gun in the bedroom and one in the family room. Again, it goes back to visualization. Where do you and your family spend most of your time? If it's the kitchen or family room, you'll want a gun there. Many people think of having a gun in their bedroom, but what if the intruder cuts you off before you get upstairs? Look at your house and visualize where family spends the most time. Also, hide mace and panic buttons around house. The gun(s) you choose should, if possible, be the same or similar model that you are familiar with.

How long should your gun last? If it is properly cleaned and maintained, it will last forever. You might want something with a more modern design, but you don't need to change guns over time. You just want to make sure you can still use it comfortably if your physical capabilities change.

The decision to bring a firearm into the equation concerning your cache of options is a very serious one. Selection of the right-for-you firearm is going to take time and effort. If you do put the time in, it will pay you dividends in the end. Don't let someone tell you that you only need one gun. The correct equation for this is $Gt = Gp + 1$, with Gt meaning the total needed and Gp meaning the number you currently possess. Therefore, the total number of firearms you need is always one more than the amount you currently own.

CHAPTER
13

Gun Storage

Gun storage and one's particular needs are something that is very personal. What works for you may not work for me. Something else you need to keep in mind is that each state has their own storage laws, and it is up to you to know them. Beyond what is lawful, you have a moral obligation to keep your firearm inaccessible from unauthorized persons and children. When you are shopping for a safe, do your research. Online, you can find all kinds of reviews and even videos of people trying to break into different gun storage options. Just make sure you have found reliable sources. There are two types of storage options we need to talk about here: long-term and quick access.

Long-term

This would be the type of storage that is inaccessible completely. Your guns are in a safe and unloaded. Storage like this is easy to find. All you need to do is invest in a fireproof safe. But it must be inaccessible from people's eyes. You don't want people to be able to see this, as guns can be an attractive item to steal. Safes just scream, "I have valuable stuff in me."

If you have this type of safe, you'll also want to keep your ammunition locked in it. Ammunition is unsafe to be left around, even if it's not in a gun. It can't be around children. Your kids shouldn't bring ammunition to school for "show and tell," should they stumble upon it. You don't want to get those kinds of calls from your school's principal's office, or worse yet, in this day and age, the police.

Your gun safe can also be used to store important documents, jewelry, or anything you want to take extra good care of and keep secure. But this type of safe is not for quick and easy access, and don't expect it to be! You can get a fireproof safe for anywhere from $300 to $30,000. There are small ones available if you live in a small apartment. The options are endless. Second floor heavy safes are dangerous for a number or reasons. The floor structure may not support the weight once it is loaded and, if there is a fire, the safe could fall through the floor.

I generally don't recommend display cases. They are not a safe, and they are not secure. They are usually glass. Even if they are tempered glass, they are breakable. Some display cases will run cable to the wall so the guns can't be pulled out. A general rule of thumb is that the more decorative a case is, the less secure it is. This is not my style nor my recommendation.

One other thing to remember on storage: Any guns that you have in the house that are not for immediate access should have a trigger lock or be locked in a safe. Every gun that is sold in the US comes with a trigger or cable lock. Every police department has them for free. Most ranges also have them. Project Childsafe®, a program with the National Shooting Sports Foundation, will also supply these trigger locks free of charge. There is absolutely no excuse not to have a trigger lock on any of your firearms.

You don't want to keep a firearm in too dry or too humid a location. The NRA recommends a 70-degree fahrenheit temperature and 50 percent relative humidity, although I prefer closer to 35 percent relative humidity, since steel can start to rust over 50 percent. Also, if you keep your firearms in a colder environment and take them quickly to a warmer space, light condensation can form between the firearm and your hand.

Quick access

If you are buying a gun for self-defense, you'll want to have storage that offers quick access. A gun won't do you much good if you can't get to it when you need it.

My favorite lock box has a Simplex lock on it. It usually has a four-digit code that you can input. You should be opening that safe every single day, 365 days a year...More on that later.

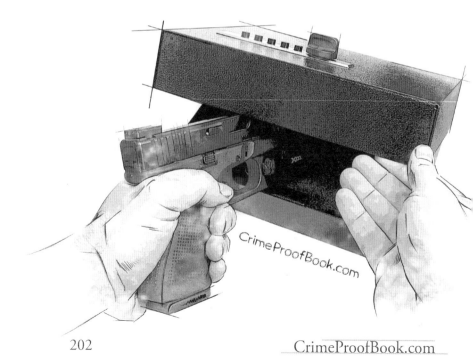

I am not a fan of anything with batteries for gun storage. Batteries are a dangerous proposition. They can die at the worst possible time, and probably will. You'll also see a lot of biometric safes that can read your fingerprints. I'm not a fan of them either, because I don't think the technology is there yet. The problem with them is that, if you cut your finger, if you're sweaty, bloody or trembling, then there's a good chance that the fingerprint reader won't work. Just think about trying to unlock your cell phone with your fingerprint and how well that goes all the time. You won't be locked out of your email or social media apps; you'll be locked out of your last resort self-defense tools!

There is also a new evolution of safes that are hooked up through phone apps. I'm not a fan of them either. My mantra is, if it can fail, it will. These lock boxes that can be accessed via a mobile device have unexplored potential for hacking. I also don't like storage with keys. Your kids will figure out what that key is for and how to get into the gun box. Further, keys are cumbersome, especially in a high-stress situation. If you must have one of the hi-tech safes, make sure you know where the backup keys are and that they are secure from unwanted users.

The brand I have is a V-line storage box. It's heavy gauge steel and very well made. I've had the same two boxes for 25 years. They are all mechanical and have served me well.

Where do you put this storage box? You want to have immediate access. Again, use visualization and mindset. Where do you spend most of your time? Bedroom, garage, or living room area? Wherever you are the most is where your gun should be stored. If you have more than one gun and more than one safe, all of them should have the same code.

Here's what I do: I have my primary safe in my bedroom, bolted into a drawer. My safe contains my gun, flashlights, a light stick with my house key, and my vitamins. Vitamins? Why? Remember how I said before that you should open this safe every single day? You take a vitamin every single day, right? This is a reason to open that safe every single day. Why is that so important? You want muscle memory to kick in. When you are in a dangerous situation, you probably won't be calm. If your muscles simply know what to do, you'll be able to get that safe open quickly.

I'm a big advocate of safes like this being bolted to a drawer in the nightstand. We should be doing everything we can to make it harder for criminals to leave with the safe. Further, when these boxes are bolted down, they are much harder to break into.

Another thought is to go to a place like New Jersey Concealment Furniture. They sell furniture with a safe in it. If you have no kids in the house, they build furniture with

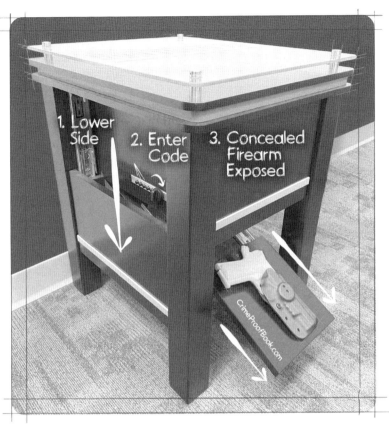

1. Lower Side
2. Enter Code
3. Concealed Firearm Exposed

a secret compartment. There are a whole host of options when it comes to concealment furniture, and the sky is the limit. Wall art, end tables, coffee tables, flag cases, clocks, etc. have all been made into secure concealment furniture. You need to find what is right for you and your situation. Secrecy is key when it comes to concealment options!

When your gun is in the safe, it should be loaded with home defense ammunition, namely hollow point cartridges (make sure they are legal where you live). You should have a minimum of two speed loaders with the gun (if it's a revolver) and two flashlights, as well as your light stick with your house key on it. Have at least three extra magazines full of ammunition if you have a semi-automatic gun. Every daylight savings time, you should switch the magazines in the gun because the springs can get "tired" after a while; they have "memory." If you do opt for an electronic box, change the batteries at the same time, when you do all your other daylight savings time chores. The round in the chamber should also be cycled out when you swap magazines.

What condition should you keep your home defense firearm in? Unloaded, loaded magazine detached from the firearm, loaded magazine in the firearm without a round in the chamber, or loaded magazine and chamber? If you choose the latter, loaded with a round in the chamber, I recommend keeping it in a pocket holster so that the trigger is covered and the weapon is easy to draw. Further, you can store it in your pocket if necessary. This is especially of importance when/if the police arrive; you do not want to be standing there with a gun in your hand. Keep in mind, no revolvers have safeties, and once you cock the hammer on a revolver, which significantly reduces the force required to pull the trigger, you have no method to safe the weapon other than manually lowering the hammer on a live round.

Gun storage is a very personal topic. You need to find the options that work best for you and your living arrangement. Know that there may be certain statutory requirements on how you store your firearm. Beyond the law, you have a moral obligation to keep firearms out of the hands of children and those who are unauthorized.

CHAPTER

14

Using Your Gun

The aftermath

If you must use your gun, you should call 911 and tell them someone's in your house. You provide your address, describe the situation, tell them what you're wearing, what the intruder is wearing, and give as much detail as possible. Repeat your address and try to stay as calm as possible. If you're holed up in a bedroom, tell them the locations of your family. You must act in a calm and methodical manner. Remember, not only are you giving important information to the authorities, but you are also creating evidence which can be called back during a trial, should you find yourself in one. Note, our 911 call system was designed for landline phones many years ago. When you call 911 from a cell phone, make sure you say your address two times clearly and concisely so that officers can be dispatched even if the bad guy knocks your phone out of your hand. My cell phone is a business phone and the address is at the range, not my house. Imagine the police showing up there instead?

If someone starts to approach you and you have to use your firearm, tell them, "Don't move, please leave, I have a gun and I will use it." Use command words. Remember, distance is your best friend.

One thing you need to remember: we never shoot to kill, and we never shoot to wound. We shoot to stop the threat. We keep shooting until the threat stops.

Now you've had to use the gun. The first thing you have to do is secure the scene and area. What if there's a gun, a knife, or multiple attackers? What do you do with your gun? Do you put it down while you let the police in? No. You do not put your gun down until the police arrive. Remember, all of this is happening in a matter of seconds.

You cannot touch or alter the crime scene. What if you're kneeling down, the bad guy comes in, they see a gun and turn to flee, but you shoot anyway? At this point, you did what you did. It's over. Leave it alone. Don't touch the crime scene. If the gun is still near the bad guy, they could still hurt you. Stay on the phone line with 911, keep the family away, continue to keep your gun trained on the person, and keep barking commands. Try and position the intruder with their head closest to you and legs far away.

Sometimes intruders will comply. If you have two people in your house, keep a distance between the two of them. They will be begging you to let them go. Don't do it. All bets are off at this point. You were violated and deserve justice. Have the police take care of the situation when they arrive, and insist on pressing charges.

What do you do with a gun when the police arrive? You must secure your gun without increasing your risk from the criminal(s) or the responding police officers. Raise your hands with your palms facing them so they can see you have nothing in your hands. They will need to sort the scene out. Expect to be handcuffed. They will decide later who to uncuff. You will want to talk to police, but don't. That's not your job at that moment. Your first priority is yours and your family's health and safety. Tell the police, "I want to comply fully. But I'm experiencing chest pains, shortness of breath, and I need medical attention." We don't need you to die at this point if you have a condition and are experiencing such symptoms. Oh, and by the way, once you request medical treatment, the police can't question you. Given that, consider any "symptom" you might be having as potentially life threatening.

Don't submit to interrogation until you have legal representation. The police aren't there to be your friends. If you say, "I didn't mean to shoot him," you've just admitted to something. Once you meet with your attorney, they will be with you when you are questioned. They probably won't file charges against you if you have legal representation.

Attorneys are not attached to the situation in any way. Tell them exactly what happened. Tell them the truth. Spill the beans 100%. If the person turned and you shot them, tell your attorney that. Then your attorney will develop a plan of how you're going to answer the cops. You will fare much better if you tell the truth to your legal representative.

Dealing with the police and asserting your rights

It is important to understand how to deal with the police. Even though honest gun owners generally support the police and believe that the "police are your friend," complying with the police instead of "lawyering up" can cause major legal problems for the law-abiding citizen.

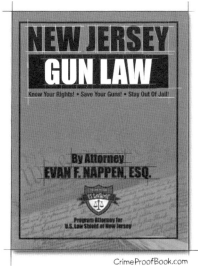

NEW JERSEY GUN LAW

Know Your Rights! • Save Your Guns! • Stay Out Of Jail!

By Attorney
EVAN F. NAPPEN, ESQ.

Program Attorney for
U.S. Law Shield of New Jersey

CrimeProofBook.com

Below is sage advice from Attorney Evan Nappen. Read it carefully and remember to follow it no matter how innocent you are!

S.A.C.

A Strategic Air Command (SAC) base provided the nuclear-based defense to the United States from 1946 – 1992 (many of you aren't quite old enough to remember). If stopped or arrested by law enforcement on a weapons violation, the S.A.C. Constitutional mnemonic provides a basic legal defense foundation for the honest gun owner:

S – Remain SILENT

– "I assert my right to remain silent."

A – ASK for your Attorney

– "I want my/an attorney."

C – Do NOT CONSENT

to any search. Do not make or sign any statements without your attorney's approval.

ALWAYS be RESPECTFUL, POLITE, and COOPERATIVE. DO NOT PHYSICALLY RESIST under any circumstances!

You will have to REMAIN SILENT, and YOU MUST REASSERT YOUR REQUEST FOR AN ATTORNEY over and over again during the arrest and interrogation process. DO NOT RELENT!

Remember: SAC

#1: Remain SILENT
(The "S" in SAC)

The Fifth Amendment protection against self-incrimination, also known as the "Right to Remain Silent," is one of the most important Constitutional protections Americans have that many other countries do not grant. Yet naive people in the United States routinely ignore Fifth Amendment protections and bury themselves with "explanations." When it comes to a criminal violation, most law-abiding citizens are ignorant about the details of the law and its many loopholes and defenses. By opening their mouths, they remove all doubt about their ignorance and usually give the State something not just to use against them, but to twist against them.

By remaining silent, a person avoids: inadvertently incriminating oneself, wiping out potential legal defenses, and assisting the State in its often unjustified case. ALWAYS remain silent after being arrested for any reason. Remaining silent is the purest form of a self-protection. Remember the old saying: The fish that opens its mouth is the one that gets caught!

If you are stopped or accosted by a Law Enforcement Officer and asked any question, your first response should be "Am I free to go?" If the response is "Yes," then walk away. If the response is "No," then you are in custody and the above rights apply, and you then respond by saying, "I assert my right to remain silent and want to speak to my attorney." (See below under #3 for the exception if you are stopped in your vehicle).

#2: ASK for your ATTORNEY
(The "A" in SAC)

The Sixth Amendment guarantees an individual's right to an attorney. By asking for your/an attorney and remaining silent, honest gun owners provide themselves with a fundamental foundation for a strong legal defense. Defense attorneys smile when they learn their clients stood firm on their rights. Say, "I want my attorney." If you do not already have an attorney, say, "I want an attorney."

Requesting an attorney does much more than simply getting the accused legal counsel. Simply requesting an attorney causes a wall of constitutional protection to spring up. This wall prevents further interrogation by the authorities. After demanding an attorney, statements obtained from further interrogation made without the defendant's attorney present cannot be used by the State as evidence, as long as the person continues to verbally ask for an attorney. This holds true unless defendants foolishly waive their right to an attorney (see rule #3 below). The Sixth Amendment protections often apply even if information is obtained by "dirty tricks," without one's attorney being present.

Recent court decisions require you to reassert your request for an attorney at every opportunity where you are asked a question. DO NOT relent. Continue to remain silent and ask for your attorney.

#3: Do not CONSENT to waiving ANY rights (The "C" in SAC)

A right given up is a right lost. DO NOT CONSENT TO A SEARCH WITHOUT A WARRANT. DO NOT SIGN ANY STATEMENTS WITHOUT

AN ATTORNEY'S ADVICE. All citizens have a Fourth Amendment right to a warrant being issued before their person or premises are searched. There are exceptions to the necessity for a warrant and there is a large body of law that exists as to when law enforcement officers have justification or probable cause for a warrantless search. However, whether an exception for the warrantless search exists or not, YOU SHOULD NEVER CONSENT TO A WARRANTLESS SEARCH.

The key here is consent. If a law enforcement officer insists on searching you, DO NOT RESIST being searched. Just make it verbally clear that you are not consenting to this search; say "I do not consent to this search." Additionally, do not sign any consent form without the advice of your attorney. In some cases, the officer may be allowed to ask you to sign that you received the summons. This is done so that you don't have to be formally arrested. Additionally, if stopped while driving, you may be required by law to produce your driver's license, registration, and insurance card. Refusal of blood alcohol testing is usually unlawful as well. Check your jurisdiction's law for specifics.

If a search is done without adequate probable cause, then the court will suppress evidence obtained after a hearing handled by your attorney, and the State will not be able to use it. When people consent to a search, then anything found may be used as evidence—evidence against them—whether there was probable cause or not! Although law-abiding citizens may feel that they have nothing to hide, consider that people may nonetheless possess contraband that they otherwise believed to be legal, or that others may have left or planted in their cars, in their houses, or even in their clothing.

NOT giving consent is NOT probable cause for a search. Some people feel that if they do not consent to the search, the officer will suspect them. People are afraid of the inappropriate question: "What do you have to hide?" The actual legal question, which must be answered by the State at court, is: "Why did this law enforcement officer feel it was necessary to invade your privacy and conduct a search?" This question properly shifts the burden of proof to the police, as was our Founding Fathers' intention. Remember, the Fourth Amendment is there to protect our privacy from government intrusion.

I am frequently asked by law abiding citizens about what to do when pulled over in a vehicle while transporting firearms. There are two basic steps. First of all, make sure that all items are being transported lawfully. And secondly, be polite and respectful; hopefully the reason for your pullover is simply a traffic matter and will be handled as such without it blowing up into a full-fledged car/person search. The key indicator as to whether this stop is going further than a potential traffic summons will be revealed by the officer's questions and actions.

If asked whether or not there are any weapons in the car, immediately be aware that you are in danger of becoming a victim of the gun laws. This question may be handled in many ways. However, my personal response is to ask the officer why I am being asked that question. The answer to this question goes directly to the issue of probable cause. Why are you being asked whether you have weapons in the car? Is this simply a fishing expedition on behalf of the officer, or is it because a weapon is in plain view on the front seat? If it is a fishing expedition, then that question is clearly unjustified. If there is a gun or ammunition on the seat, then regardless of your answer, you are probably looking at having your vehicle and person searched. The key here is not to give any excuses for a vehicle search (e.g., items left in plain view, expired motor vehicle licenses, odd behaviors, etc). If you obey the law and act in a practical and intelligent manner, you should be able to avoid vehicle/person searches.

The bottom line

We have all heard the Miranda Rights given on various TV cop shows and movies. We have heard them so often that many folks do not even pay attention to what these rights truly mean. The media has so belittled our Constitutional Rights that many naive citizens simply ignore them. Gun owners cannot afford to ignore them. Always remain polite and respectful when asserting your rights, but the key is to assert them. Do not be embarrassed or intimidated into giving up your rights. If you give up your rights (apart from making your attorney's job defending you that much tougher), you will have substantially increased your chance of becoming the next horror story gun law victim that your friends will be talking about while you sit in jail.

Remember, do not fall for the media desensitizing us to our rights. It is unfortunate that our rights are not taught in our schools. One would think something as important as that would be a priority, but if everybody knew their rights and stood on their rights, the government would not be able to act in the heavy-handed manner that it currently does. Do not fall for the trap that has been set by those out to dilute and make ineffective our Constitutional Rights. Stand on your rights! Millions of men and women have died and sacrificed for these rights; show them the respect that they deserve by standing on your rights and not foolishly waiving them.

It is also advisable to have a criminal defense attorney on call in case you need one. There are a number of legal protection plans available for gun owners to protect themselves in which an attorney is available 24 hours a day, seven days a week, should you have an emergency. One of the best programs is US Law Shield, which provides, among other benefits, a hotline to reach an attorney at any time. If you belong to such a program, you can immediately say "I want to speak to my attorney" and have an attorney to actually speak with, who can then assert your rights and act as a shield between you and the government. Any time the government wants to get in your life, you should have an attorney to act between you and the government. One last tip. Anytime someone says, "You don't need an attorney," that is a surefire sign that you need one!

CHAPTER
15
Online and Digital Security

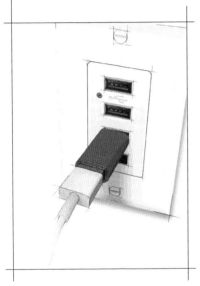

It's the 21st century, and there is close to no way to avoid technology, the internet, online banking, etc. For many, social media is a necessary part of their lives—this is also the case for many small businesses. The internet and social media have become the modern-day town square. Not only is this the forum for expression and information exchange, but the square is flanked by all the businesses one may need to visit. Threats to the security of your information and physical well-being are prevalent in our confusing digital world.

The digital world

You have to be careful because scammers are out there 24/7, especially from foreign countries, trying to get personal data, passcodes, and anything else you have that's supposed to be secure. There are things you can do to avoid this. For example, don't post a picture while at an airport when you're on your way to go on vacation. Then people will know that your house is empty for a week or two. While away, don't post those pictures either. Wait until you get home if you feel the need to share such information.

Phishing scams are something that you need to be aware of. Phishing are those instances I mentioned concerning someone trying to obtain your personal information and/or passwords to online accounts. An entity that employs deceptive techniques to mask their identity and try to trick people are generically called Catfish. The term "Catfish" concerns luring someone into a relationship online, and that doesn't just mean romantic. Regardless, you need to be vigilant on who you accept into your digital life and what information you give them. My advice is, do not accept people you do not know as "friends" on any of your private social media accounts. Phishing scams are very hard to tell from legitimate emails from companies and entities we all normally do business with. If you receive an "urgent" email from, let's say, your credit card company, who's looking for account verification or you will have your card suspended, please read it over carefully before responding. Go around the email and call the card company directly and see if it is in fact legitimate.

Spam is a big problem today. Just like the phishing schemes, spammers are out in full force. No, a Nigerian prince is not leaving you their estate, making you instantly rich. That is not happening, no, no, no. Your best course of action when dealing with spam is to just mark it as spam and delete it. Don't reply, that only confirms your email address is valid and thus a sellable commodity.

And did you know, the number one password that people use is "Password." The number two is "Password1." Don't do this. Use strong passwords. If you use shared computers, maybe at work, remember to clear out your browsing history and cache before leaving the PC. You don't want to leave websites logged in or have passwords remembered on any shared computers. This will leave you vulnerable to having your information stolen. You can also look into getting a password manager—you download the App and start changing passwords, and it works across all of your devices and offers great protection.

Any accounts that you have that allow for two-factor authentication, make sure you take advantage of that. It's another level of security for you. For example, when our IT guy here at the range logs into anything, I get a notification and I have to approve it. I know what is going on with my accounts at all times this way.

Another thing people should consider is to use a unique email for online shopping accounts. I have one email that I use anytime I purchase something online. When I get an email from that account, I know to research further, especially if it's not a purchase I recall making.

When you're online shopping, use one dedicated credit card only for online purchases. This does two things for you: one, you can monitor purchases. And two, if something happens, you only have to cancel one credit card, not a whole lot of them.

Whenever possible, use secure networks to log into the internet. Public Wi-Fi can grab all your personal information, which is a goldmine for scammers. Be careful when charging your device in a public place. You can buy a data blocker for charging your phone in public places. It's a small device that you plug into your charger, which makes it so that your phone will charge, but your data can't be hacked into. They cost about $5 a piece on Amazon, and they can save you from a world of trouble.

The problem is, people get too comfortable and figure anything is safe. It's Condition White. You figure that nothing has ever happened to you, and it probably won't. The next thing you know, you're on vacation in a

Data blockers
stop hackers.

foreign country and someone has shifted all your money out of your account.

Here's yet another way you can get scammed. Hackers have been known to go to a local post office and change your mailing address. They will show fictitious identification to make it look like you are moving. By the time this happens, it could be months before you realize that your data has been stolen because you're not getting any of your bills. But your credit cards will have racked up massive debt that you are responsible for if you don't report the card lost or stolen.

You, the internet, and your information

Something else that I recommend people do concerning their online information is scour the internet for your name and address. Use search engines to see what is out there about you. In many instances there are sites that list your known associates, family members, you name it, and your information could be out there for grabs. While much of what is out there is "public" info, why make it easy for people who wish to inflict harm on you by having it that easy to grab? Go through these sites and see about having your information removed. There is no reason why we should leave our information out in the open. Some search engines have alert features, and you can have an email sent to you every time a certain search term gets entered. There are also services available that will, for a fee, scrub your name and address from the internet more efficiently than you could. New products and services become available every day, so do your research before signing up for one.

What you put out on the internet is forever. Yup. Don't think you can just delete something and it'll be gone, because it won't. Something called the "way back machine" or internet archive at archive.org is out there. In short, people can use this tool to look at anything that was ever online. Recently, a friend of mine had his mind blown when another friend showed him something he wrote on a secure message board back in 1999. That message board has been defunct for over 20 years, but the guy knew where to look and what to look for. As luck would have it, the message that was archived was not derogatory or negative, but nonetheless, something that was "deleted" over 20 years ago still exists.

The idea and concept of this is important for many different reasons. Aside from having potentially embarrassing things about you out there, what if you had something posted once upon a time and it got entered as evidence in a court case? Anything and everything you post online, on social media, etc. can and will be used against you for whatever reason you could imagine, especially if you have to defend yourself and have charges levied against you.   Remember all of this before you hit the send button. If you do go through your social media accounts to scrub out any likes, posts, or comments you have made, just remember that they may come back to haunt you one day anyhow! My advice is to keep a low profile on the internet.

Online marketplaces

A big thing that everyone has been getting into these days is buying and selling things online. With auction sites becoming a thing, we now live in a giant virtual flea market. With that comes local sales sites, where you find what you're looking for and pick up the item from the seller. A lot of really cool stuff can be found in these marketplaces and, if you look hard enough, a lot of stuff is given away for free. Any time there is the potential for commerce, there is the potential for being ripped off.

To cover and list every type of scam and scheme out there would be a whole chapter in and of itself. If you are going to engage in shopping in digital marketplaces, there are a few things you should do to safeguard yourself. Take, for example, a friend of mine who bought some tables, then we'll break the exchange down.

My buddy wanted to get new end tables for his house. He took to a social media site marketplace and found a woman selling tables that he liked who lived only one town over. He made contact and the woman was very quick to reply. Once they decided on a price, my buddy asked her for her phone number, so he could call her for all the details. They spoke on the phone and set up a time, date, and location for pickup. He wrote down the name she had on her profile along with the phone number and address of the woman. When he picked up the tables, he was greeted by a retirement aged woman at her home. She lived in a smaller retirement community that had many attached houses and shared driveways. He introduced himself to her and she let him into her house. My buddy paid the lady and packed the tables up into his car. Before leaving, he struck up a dialog with her:

"Just curious, have you been selling a lot of stuff online?" to which she replied, "No, not at all. This was my first time, and it was so easy." This made my buddy raise his eyebrows a bit. "Did anyone know that I was coming over to your house?" She said "No, I mean, I told my girlfriend I was going to sell the tables online and she thought it was a good idea, that was all. Why?"

What proceeded was a lecture. My friend explained to her what she did wrong and how to protect herself if she was going to be doing this type of thing again.

First, always do your best to verify that who you are talking to online is who they say they are. Yes, even over the phone, people can pretend to be someone else. But asking for a phone number and demanding to talk to someone prior to them meeting with you will usually weed out any scammers. What information you do get, write it down and leave it with a loved one. If you are going to a location, leave the address, name, and phone number of the contact. Email it, write it on an envelope, whatever. Let your loved ones know who you are having come to pick something up or who you are going to pick something up from. Should something happen to you, there will be some leads. Take screenshots of the person's profile picture, etc. If you are selling something, let your loved ones know the same information: who is coming over, their presumed name, number, and yes, profile pictures. If you can, have someone else with you at home if you're having them come there to pick up goods. Have a weapon on you and ready for use if need be. Be prepared to call the police in a hurry if you need to. Do not let people into your garage or house unless absolutely necessary. You could be getting cased out by whoever is buying your stuff.

If you are selling something and it's not very big, meet in a public place that has security cameras. Better yet, call your local police department. Many of them have safe online sale exchange sites set up on their property. They are under video surveillance, and the police are right there. In any and every event, you should always suggest meeting at the local police department to the person you are doing business with, just to feel them out. If they sound hesitant or shaky about meeting you there to buy your video game system or something, then forget it. Don't do business with that person.

Just because you meet someone on the internet who wants to buy your old TV stand, don't get all excited and click your heels because you'll be rid of it and make a buck...they can be a scammer. Sometimes it's cheaper and in your best interest to just throw certain items out or give directly to Goodwill for a tax write-off. Try to use private groups that are local to you, and keep exchanges public so that, at minimum, there is a record of who is interested. Once you establish contact, then go into private messages, and always confirm with them over the phone.

This only scratches the surface on buying and selling goods online. Take a few moments to really think about the process and what the implications are. It is a very lucrative business, ripping people off while engaging in any commerce online.

Online dating safety

So, I am guilty of using online dating apps. Even though it was me, a male meeting females, I was still on full guard and was overly cautious the entire date. When setting up a profile on dating sites, use a Google phone number that cannot be tracked to you. Use photos that are not taken off your social media pages, because criminals can use a Google search to find your real identity. You should also do a search of yourself online and see what is posted about you on the first few search pages. Remember, criminals rely on confidence. If I saw a post of the woman

I was going to meet that revealed that she was at last year's German Shepard rescue event, I would bring up in conversation that German Shepards are my favorite dog. This is to make her think we are a great match to further gain her confidence and have her drop her guard sooner. I can find many examples of this type of information on most people in a public search.

When meeting, make sure it is a public place. The female should always pick the location, and the female should always arrive early to case out the place. She should sit in a highly visible location, not a dark corner booth, for example. If you must drink, have no more than one alcoholic beverage during the date, and you must keep your drink and water glass close to you the entire time. If you get up to use the restroom, you should not eat or drink anything that is left on the table when you return, so plan accordingly. This is the perfect time for your drink or food to get spiked. Take no chances.

Make sure a minimum of two people know your location, etc. Call or text them when you arrive and as you are being seated. There are also tracking apps that you can share with two people so they can keep an eye on your whereabouts.

After the date, make sure you do not get escorted back to your vehicle and do not ever take a ride back from your first date! You control the situation. If the person is caring, they will understand the precautionary steps you are taking. If they do not understand or get aggravated by these steps, cut them loose now.

These steps should be followed until you feel you have enough confidence with your new friend, but of course never fully let your guard down for a long time.

Keep your family safe

Something that, as guardians, we need to be aware of with our kids is the subject of online bullying and what they are doing. This is a very real and dangerous situation that is going on today. There is close to nothing "social" about social media, and yet we are all drawn to it, looking for small endorphin spikes from likes and shares. Children are no different, and are very susceptible to falling into such acceptance from their peers. The long-term effects of social media use have yet to be fully discovered, but what has become acutely clear is that kids are suffering from things that occur in the digital world. Not only do we have to be worried about and aware of who our kids are talking to, but we also need to make sure they are not feeling alienated or abused by others in the digital arena. Instances of youth suicide have spiked from this new dynamic, and we need to protect our children. These are things you need to keep in mind. Remember, kids have become victims of sex traffickers and all sorts of other bad things because of cyber bullying.

Always know the passwords to any devices you give your children. Tell your kids that, since you are paying for the device, you get to know what's going on at all times. Then monitor their accounts. Make sure they don't change their passwords on you. If everything seems legit, don't mention it to your child. They will forget you are monitoring them. But if you see something, then you have to take action. You should also make sure you have a tracker app or option activated on your children's cell phones at all times as well.

Your cell phone

Cell phones are part of our day-to-day lives. In many ways they have almost completely replaced the computer for some people. You store and have a lot of data on your cell phone, so you must safeguard that. Keeping things like screen lock passwords are important to keep people out of your personal business. Also, features that would allow you to track your phone from another device, send it messages, and completely shut it down if need be, should be enabled. Should you get separated from your phone by losing it or it being stolen, these tools could come in handy to recover your property.

Don't use pet names for your significant other in your phone. Here's why: let's say a criminal steals your phone and wallet. You have your husband listed as Babe. The criminal will text Babe and say something like, "Hey, I forgot the ATM password. What is it?" Babe will text you back, and now the criminal has your debit card and password. Field day! If you list everyone in your phone by their proper names, the criminal won't know who to text.

Your safety and security does not end in the physical world. Good, bad, or indifferent, we also live in a digital universe. The online world has the power to communicate powerful ideas, has been behind revolutions in countries, and has connected people all over the world for good and noble purposes. Remember that any time there is an arena where someone has something to gain, there is always going to be someone that tries to take advantage!

CHAPTER
16
Senior Security

With the baby boom generation well into the waning years of their lives, we need to remember them. Like children, the elderly are easy prey, gullible, and not always physically able to take care of themselves. Elder abuse and silver alerts have entered into our society front and center. The loved ones that raised us and/or had a part of molding us into who we are today need to be safeguarded and protected too.

Today people are living longer, and two things can happen. We either lose physical or mental abilities.

Some people will lose both. Sometimes it happens fast, sometimes incrementally over time. Whatever the case, crimes against seniors are a great market for criminals. Scams have happened that get elderly people to give their credit card numbers out over the phone. Older people with decreased mobility are physically easier to rob. Those that have cognitive issues are especially vulnerable.

A current scam that has been around for a while is the grandparent scam. Someone calls the house in the middle of the night and says, "Grandpa, it's Johnny. I got arrested and I need bail money. I don't want mom and dad to know. Can you help me?" And without checking, grandpa will be upset that his grandson is in trouble and give his credit card number out.

We need to educate the elderly about scams. Criminals look for easy opportunities, so we have to look for ways to remove those opportunities. As people lose their alertness, it's hard for you to protect them, especially when you're not there. It's your job to teach them that there are lots of scams online or through the phone. Try to tell your parents to get information if someone calls them, and then to call you and let you vet it before they call them back. They may be reluctant, but if a little part registers in their brain, you could save them and yourself a lot of trouble.

The grandparents of a friend of mine fell victim to one such scam. His grandfather had mobility and other health issues. Being a veteran, he heavily relied on the VA for many things. One day, two women posing as therapists from the VA showed up to his home. They told him that they were there to help him with his walking and had some therapies to administer. My friend's grandmother was doing her thing, cooking and cleaning, little old Italian lady—this was in Brooklyn. One of the women got to massaging and "working" his grandfather's legs while the other slipped into the bedroom. A day later, my friend's grandmother found a substantial amount of cash was stolen from them. She was old school and kept thousands of dollars of cash in the house…neatly stowed in the top drawer of her dresser, protected by stretched out granny panties and exhausted bras from the flapper era. The multiple elements of this crime should be thought about by you, the reader. Someone tipped these ladies off about my friend's grandfather's VA status and mobility issues. They worked in pairs and knew what they were doing. This is not fiction, this really happened. My buddy's grandparents were not only embarrassed, but they were ripped off of over ten thousand dollars.

Other issues with your older family members that you have to think about are personal safety issues for them. Look around the house your loved ones live in and take away anything that could be harmful to them. You have to senior-proof houses. It's a reality. If you have kids, think back to baby proofing your own home. Well, now you need to do the same to your older family members' homes.

Have you ever seen your 94-year-old father up on the ladder getting leaves out of the gutters? You have to take the ladder away! It's either that or you may end up getting a call that your dad just took a fall from a 15-foot ladder. As we age, we don't necessarily accept it. With that, people will try to continue to do things that they've always done. In many cases, they can't. Older seniors sometimes pass out, and many doctors that I have spoken to tell me that there is no specific reason that it happens. What does often happen is that they hit their heads when they fall. Buy the person that you are concerned about a bicycle helmet and encourage them to wear it. It could be the difference between being stunned and cracking their head open.

To keep your parents safe, you can get a couple of cameras that have alerts as to when there is movement in the house. These serve two purposes. You can monitor for movement that shouldn't be happening. You can also make sure that movement is happening. What happens if the camera hasn't shown movement in several hours? Maybe your mother has fallen, and she needs help. Different systems can be integrated right into doorbell cams and floodlight cams, making it easy to be able to keep an eye

on your loved ones, their home, and what might be going on outside as well. With cameras inside, you have to be careful of where you place them in the house to protect your loved ones' privacy. If you get a good camera, you can hear if someone is calling for help from a distance. You don't need to put a camera in the bathroom because you'll be able to hear if they need something, even if the camera is in the next room.

Life alerts are good devices for the elderly. Your parents can wear one around their neck. You can also have emergency buttons around the house. Different alarm systems will have a medical alert function as well. You can be 3,000 miles away and keep an eye on mom or dad with these tools.

Safe at home

I like to keep everything in my parents' house locked, including the garage, basement doors, and windows. Elderly people don't remember to do this, and it makes breaking in very easy. Make sure curtains are drawn. The elderly will have lights on all over the house so they can see. If the curtains are open, anyone can see in. So make sure the curtains are drawn.

You can install a doorbell camera to see who is coming in and out of the house. You'll also want to get a wide-angle peephole for the elderly, and you may have to install a lower peephole, because we shrink as we age.

On that note, tell your parents to never open the door to strangers, even if they are wearing a company uniform. Those scams are very popular, and they prey on the elderly. People can come in to "perform a service," unlock a back door, and then their buddy can come in and clean a house out.

One of the problems with the elderly is that they become too trusting. They will let anyone into the house who has a good story. And they could be there to clean your parents out of all of their possessions. Here's what you tell your parents. If someone comes to the door with a uniform on and says they are from a utility company and they need to do an inspection, tell them that you're going call the police to verify them. If the repairman is legitimate, they will wait for the police to come. If not, they will hightail it out of there quickly. They can also verify with whatever company the person is claiming to be with, asking a representative if there is a service call for their address. Instill in them the belief that it is okay to do these types of things.

Also, remember that chain locks on doors provide a false sense of security. One swift kick and a chain lock will break a door right off its hinges. Deadbolts are the best way to go. The new electronic locks mentioned earlier on are great to consider, as they will allow you to make sure they are kept locked remotely.

Do a sweep of your elderly loved one's house. Look for their valuables, like money, jewelry, and other valuables. The person you are looking after may be reluctant to have you take their possessions for safe keeping, so securing them inside the home might be your best first option. As noted earlier, most criminals go right to top drawers, nightstands, or desks. You have to approach them and tell them to keep their valuables in a safe if they don't want you holding onto them. Work with them to try to pick a spot that would be the last place a thief would look. If there are still kids' rooms set up, put the valuables in drawers of children's bedrooms. Or get them a strongbox with a key. Another good place to hide things is under the tissue box cover of one of the long, horizontal tissue boxes. That's a great place to leave keys or valuables. A safe bolted down in the closet of an unused room is also something to consider.

You want to be sure that your parents don't leave important papers on their kitchen table. Have them put their important papers in a locking desk drawer. Criminals can take pictures of important papers on phone cameras. Don't let them write passwords on paper and keep them out on the table. That's another thing a criminal can snap a picture of. Anything that has enrollment in paperless options should be considered. Have those documents sent to an email address that you also have access to. This will not only allow you to keep tabs on your loved ones, but also will remove excess paperwork that could be a security liability.

The next thing to do is have the hard conversation with your elderly parent or loved one who manages their own finances. Say something like, "You guys are getting older. If something were to happen to you, I need to know what's going on. I want to be your backup." Then you can find out what's going on, what transactions have been made, etc. You should also ask them where their will is. Tell them you need this information to give you peace of mind. You have to make sure your parents aren't giving money to criminals.

This is a good time for you to switch your parents over to online banking. Their social security, pension, etc. should all be direct deposited. This makes it less likely for checks to be stolen in the mail, and gives them fewer trips to the bank. Yes, this one can be difficult because the elderly can be stubborn about change, but you need to assure them it's for their personal security.

Next, do an inventory of everything they have. Take pictures of their jewelry, watches, electronics, bank accounts, anything else you can think of, and put them in a folder on your computer. This will make life so much easier. You'll have all the information stored in one place if you need it, particularly if there were some sort of theft or loss event.

Once you have all the information you need, get a shredder and shred old papers in your parents' house. Older people tend to hang onto everything. It's your job to go in and clean everything up. Tell them you're doing a spring/fall cleaning and just get it done. Not only does this tidy up their space, it will remove potentially sensitive information from an uncontrolled environment. Big piles of bills and paperwork also make great fire hazards. This is a one-two punch.

On another safety note, you should never let the elderly go shopping alone. They are very vulnerable. They could be putting bags in their car, totally unaware of what is going on around them. That's a prime time for someone to mug them, steal their purse, etc. The best time for them to go grocery shopping is weekdays early in the morning. Certain stores have special senior hours as well. There's no reason to go on the weekend or at night. If they live in assisted living, get them to bring a buddy or companion to go with.

Assisted living

We're not going to dive too far into all the ins and outs of assisted living situations. There is a multitude of different types of living arrangements that people may have to consider. There is an old saying that a mother can take care of and raise five kids, but five kids can't take care of one mother. Ain't that the truth! Assisted living can come in the form of an actual facility or, in some situations, visiting helpers and/or live-in aids.

Elder abuse is the number one thing that you need to worry about. Make sure that you are using vetted and background-checked services for your loved ones. Neglect and outright physical abuse are things that the elderly could become subject to. I can go on for hours about some of the stories I have heard from friends about nightmare situations involving their loved ones and such abuse. The situations range from having loved ones ignored at night when calling for help to go to the restroom, to allowing them to stay in soiled adult diapers because it's inconvenient to take care of when out and about. In the case of in-home or visiting aids, yup, I know someone that had had his mother robbed (of cash money, of course). Ensuring that your loved one is getting the best care possible is top priority. Be sure to keep your eyes peeled for signs of physical and mental abuse.

If you find yourself in the unfortunate situation where your loved one has to be moved into some sort of facility, you need to still think about their security. You want to make your loved one's room or living area as comfortable and as nice as possible, since it's their new home, but don't bring valuables to these places. If your family member is known to wear jewelry, take it all from them. Remember my friend with the cooking and cleaning Italian grandmother? She used to wear a heavy twisted gold chain. Can you guess what happened to that when she was living in an assisted living facility? Hard to tell, it disappeared.

As your parents or loved ones age, you need to seek advice and help. Consulting an elder care attorney would be in everyone's best interest. Should your loved one have some sort of debilitating condition that will inevitably land them in some sort of a facility, you need to do your best to prepare them well in advance. These facilities prey on families and the elderly in many ways. Just do yourself a favor and talk to an elder care attorney about finances and property ownership sooner than later. This is a time-sensitive situation and subject, and beyond the scope of this book. Do some research and seek good sources of information. One resource I can recommend is a podcast series called "Parents Are Hard to Raise" by elder care expert Diane Berardi. If you have aging parents, look for this content in your podcast provider app and take in some professional advice.

Firearms and the elderly

The last thing you need to be worrying about is your elderly parents or loved ones having guns in the house. What happens if dad has all his old guns, but he is losing it? You need to know the laws in your state before you decide what to do. If you live in Texas, you can take guns and bring them to your house. If you live in New Jersey, you can't. But you can't leave them in the house if your elderly loved ones don't have all their wits about them.

You can buy trigger locks and put them on the guns. Or just take all the ammunition out of the guns. You can also tell your parents that the guns have to be locked up because of grandchildren coming to visit.

Finally, you can seek out professionals to help the elderly get rid of guns, transfer them to you, or get rid of them after a death.

As a society, we put a large emphasis on keeping our youth safe and secure. We do need to stop and think about our family members that are in their golden years. Out of sight is not out of mind, and we still have a duty to ensure that our mature family members are taken care of.

CHAPTER 17

Natural Disasters and Civil Unrest

On October 22, 2012, a tropical wave swirled from the ocean and hammered the east coast with one of the most devastating weather events of the 21st century. By October 29, the weather event became better known as Hurricane Sandy and breached the borders of New Jersey. Having lived through this horrific event, as so many have, we are provided with some very valuable learning experiences. I'm certainly thankful I don't live in an area where "hurricane season" is something I need to deal with on a yearly basis. Let's talk about natural disasters.

Emergency preparedness is key to your and your family's survival during any type of natural or, for that matter, man-made disaster. By now, you should have put serious thought into hardening your home and being prepared for different threats to your hearth and home. Concepts and ideas previously covered will also help you in preparation for the unknown.

The most immediately felt inconvenience during one of these events could be power outages. This is usually the first thing that will plague people during a disaster. Not having electricity for short or extended periods of time can range in severity, depending on your mindset and preparedness. What you do to be ready can be the

Hand crank USB charger and flashlight.

Hand crank radio, charger, light that never needs batteries.

CrimeProofBook.com

difference between inconvenience and life-threatening, depending on the situation.

You should have multiple flashlights as well as a huge stockpile of batteries and cyalume light sticks. Candles and matches should be stockpiled as well. You should also have an emergency radio. I have one with a hand crank that never needs batteries. I also have a USB charger with a hand crank and/or one that can be charged via solar power. There are also on the market all kinds of "jump" or "power" packs that you would use to jumpstart a car. They arc basically large battery packs, and most of them will have integrated inverters that allow you to plug in some low amperage devices. Consider getting one of those and keeping it charged. You can also go online and find little LED lanterns on the cheap. Keeping a few of those around, alongside tons of extra batteries, would be prudent. You will really appreciate these tips if there is a lengthy period with no electricity.

I love light sticks! I keep a few hundred on hand and, during Sandy, every night I would crack a few and place them around the house and on the stairs. They let off a soft glow, so you do not need to carry a flashlight, and they last about 12 hours.

If you have a generator, please be careful of carbon monoxide poisoning and where you place it next to the house. You should also secure the generator with a locked chain or cable. Many were stolen at night during Hurricane Sandy. Remember to test and run that generator monthly as well. If you purchase a portable generator and plan to connect it to your electric panel, make sure that it is done by a licensed electrician. If you turn on the back-fed generator while the house is still on commercial power, there could be a fire or an explosion.

Make sure you fill your vehicle gas tanks!

If there is a warning of a natural disaster or civil unrest, make sure all the fuel tanks for your vehicles are filled up, in case you need to make a fast exit. You can also siphon gas out of the car to run a generator if needed.

During Sandy, there were very few gas stations that had generators; therefore, there were very few stations able to supply gas. Many people would wait hours just to fill up their tank. On the Garden State Parkway, there were cars off on the shoulder for miles waiting in line in order to fill up at rest stops. Instances of stabbings and other violence broke out at gas stations during this ordeal as well.

If you do have to drive and expel fuel during some sort of a disaster, try your absolute best to have a plan

It is key to have a few bugout bags ready.

on how and where you'll refuel, and certainly minimize unnecessary travel. This is why I recommend you always keep your gas tank at least half full. If you need to bug out and beat feet, you can get a good ways away before needing to refuel.

This is a situation where it is key to have a few bugout bags as well as a stockpile of emergency food on hand. But the most important item is water! You must have at least three gallons per person per day on hand. We all have different living arrangements, whether in apartments, condos, or houses, so you need to form a storage plan that best suits your individual needs. If you're able, it would not hurt to keep a few of those five-gallon water cooler bottles in an out-of-the-way place that is cool and dark in your house.

When selecting your emergency food, you don't have to go all crazy into mega prepper mode. Whenever you go shopping, pick up an extra can or box of some food or staple that you would normally eat. If you and your kids like instant boxed mac and cheese, get a few extra boxes. If your family gobbles up cream of mushroom soup on the regular, have extra cans. You get the point. Have extra non-perishables and, as you build a stockpile, cycle out the food, eating the oldest first, then replace it with the new. While we're talking about food, you would be surprised how many homes do not have a manual can opener! Get one. Your multi-tool that I know you have and keep handy in the house and/or car may have one. These are things you need to think about.

Things like protein bars and other packaged foods are good to have on hand as well. If the shit really hits the fan, those protein bars go from being that quick snack while on a hike to instantly becoming meals! These are other items that you would want to cycle out based on any use by or purchase dates. Make sure you get varieties you like, and do work them into your normal routine, perhaps substituting a meal or two every week with one. That will help you cycle out your inventory and give you an excuse to cut down on calories a couple of times a week. I also keep four new empty five-gallon plastic gas cans at the house with a small hand siphon. You will thank me if you ever have to use them.

With power outages, you also will have heating and air conditioning outages. If whatever event happens strikes during the summer, then you suck it up and keep the windows open to stay cool. That comes with its own baggage, as you are leaving yourself vulnerable to unwanted guests. But if an event happens during the winter, well, that is a whole other ball of wax. You need to make sure you have the ability to keep yourself and your family warm. Most people will have plenty of blankets and whatnot to be able to stay warm, but if you start out cold in the first place, it's really hard to get that body temperature up. Emergency blankets and sleeping bags would not be out of the question. They are cheap and take up close to no space. You may have to have the whole family pile into one bed for everyone to stay warm. One of the most valuable things that you can have for yourself and your family members are knit hats. The majority of our body heat escapes through our heads. Wearing a hat in a cold weather situation will help keep your core warm too. I always keep a blanket, socks, gloves, scarf, and a hat in all of my vehicles.

You should always make your house look occupied to prevent thieves and looters from stopping in. You need to have eyes in the back of your head at all times. Stay inside as much as possible, and sleep in shifts if things get really bad because there are looters in the area. This is a great time to have a long gun on a sling around your neck or slung over a shoulder for protection. It allows your hands to be freed up, and nothing says "leave my property" better than a long gun! If you live in New Jersey or another state that is hostile to gun rights, you may not have a holster for your firearm. Disasters are exactly why you need a holster, so you can keep a pistol on your hip at all times in a situation like this while you're in your home.

First aid items and medication were briefly talked about in the travel section. In reality, your home safety plan should include these things, just as it should include fire extinguishers, self-defense items, etc. Like when you are traveling, having extra life-sustaining medications is paramount. If possible, keep up to a one-month supply available at all times. You should have basic first aid kits on hand too. Take this a step further and get a CPR and first aid class under your belt and your family's. Take what you learn and apply it to what you may need in your home. You don't need a trauma kit for big casualty events, but hey, it would not hurt you to have them, would it?

Another thing that is usually on the back burner but you ought to think about is entertainment. At a minimum, have a couple decks of cards, a board game or two, and maybe a book or two. If your power is out, you need to conserve what battery life you do have for any mobile devices and should not be scrolling social media or playing Candy Crush! This may not seem like an important thing, but it will keep you and your family sane if y'all are holed up together with nothing to do. If family members are freaking out, you need to keep them busy. So, if card games and Truth or Dare do not help satisfy their preoccupied minds, and you've run out of Yahtzee score cards, then take that time to reorganize the linen closet or clean the garage (if it's safe to do so). Different people will react differently in an emergency situation. You need to stay calm, keep everyone calm, and, if need be, keep everyone occupied. Unfortunately, you won't know who may or may not take well to such a situation until you are in it.

This text in no way is designed to make you a master level prepper. But the core concepts of personal security do need to be considered, especially concerning natural disasters and civil unrest. There are plenty of resources out there, and you can get as deep into emergency preparedness as you want. What is important, though, is making sure you have your basics covered! You don't want two disasters on your hands...the event and whatever happens from your failure to plan. If you are going to bug out, have a planned route and an alternate route that you have rehearsed and traveled. Have a destination in mind as well. Remember, the police probably will not respond in these times either. It does not hurt to have an ammo stockpile and soft body armor too. If you are really serious about your protection, a good set of Night Vision Goggles should also be in your kit.

CHAPTER
18

Civilian Response to an Active Shooter While Unarmed

We're going to talk about civilian response to an active shooter. This is a hot topic because we've seen over the past few years a proliferation of active shooter situations. Media coverage of these types of events does little to help the situation; in fact, they hurt it with overly obsessive coverage. One of the recent ones, as of working on this book, would be the 2017 Garden State Plaza shooting in Paramus. The shooter went into the mall, fired a few shots of an AR-15 type platform into the ceiling, then proceeded to scurry off into some corner to take his own life. We saw over 500 police officers and SWAT teams called in, and it brings to light some basic training that should be instilled in all families when going out into any public arena, venue, sporting game, or mall. What we should do is constantly and vigilantly be aware of our surroundings, and we should have a plan. When you walk into a mall with your family, you should call out a "rendezvous" point if something should happen or if you should get separated. "We all meet back here." I remember that being drilled into me when I was a child. Today I don't see parents doing it as much as it was done years ago; people have grown complacent with having mobile devices available.

If you walk into the big box store entrance of the mall near the Garden Center, you should announce to your family, friends, and loved ones, "If something should happen or someone gets separated, we'll meet back here." Now, why is this important? What if you're on one side of the mall and your loved one is on the other side of the mall, then an active shooter situation arises? How will you know if they're safe? What if they are not able to get back to you to the rendezvous point? This is why it's nice to always enter a mall or sports venue with a fully charged cell phone.

The first thing you should do if there's an active shooter is put your phone on vibrate because, if you're going to hide somewhere, you do not want your sister texting you and revealing your location so the active shooter can come over and execute you.

The next thing you should do is try to find cover if you cannot escape the mall. It's interesting because a lot of people don't know the difference between cover and concealment, which is why I've discussed this a few times throughout this book. Cover is something that could stop a bullet or protect you from some type of firepower. Concealment is something that can just cloak you or disguise you, like hiding behind a lady's clothing kiosk in the middle of the mall. That would give you concealment, but not cover. Imagine hiding behind some women's dresses, your phone goes off, and you have a weird ringtone as the active shooter is walking by. He'll now know your location, putting yourself or your family in harm's way. This is why you keep your phone on silent in such situations.

Also, when in an airport, a mall, a sports venue, etc., think about where you sit, and take note of where the emergency exits are. Take note of what your escape avenue would be. Take note of what you would bring with you. And, I've talked about this uncomfortable notion with people before; if my ex-father-in-law was with us in his wheelchair, with my two stepsons, I would probably have to leave my ex-father-in-law behind for the safety of the kids and for speed of escape.

If you look at any of the videos from the active shooter situation that happened in 2013 at the LAX airport, you'll notice that people were running in herds and were looking back to see where the noise and the shooting were coming from. This is a HUGE no-no! Whether you're in a mall, airport, or any other environment, there's no need to look back. Look forward towards your exit or safe area and keep running in that direction. Every time you turn back, you slow down and increase your chances of tripping, falling, or hurdling over someone in front of you. When you are running away, you are running towards something—safety! Not looking back! Have a plan. You're going to put yourself or your family in harm's way. DO NOT LOOK BACK! There's nothing back there for you. Safety is forward.

Okay, we have an active shooter in the mall. You've run for cover in a retail store. There are other employees in the retail store. If there's a back exit into the mall, someone should take charge and you should all hightail it out of that exit and get to safety. Hide behind cars in the parking lot. Get as far out to the outer perimeter of the location as you possibly can.

We don't know if this is a real terror threat, or if this is a renegade active shooter. We don't know what it is at this point. All we know is that we hear popping sounds and people are running for safety. If we're in a retail store and we try to escape out the back door, that might not always be feasible. Many of these stores you cannot escape. There is no back door to the parking lot, so now it's time to barricade yourself in, close the door, lock the door, pile things up in front of the door. Do whatever you can possibly do to put some cover between you and the active shooter. At this point, all lights should be off if possible (in some of these stores, the lights are on timers). You should hit the deck low to try to make yourself and your family as small a target as possible. Now, just wait it out.

In another situation, you're with your wife and she drags you into one of these candle stores. An active shooter situation occurs, the shooter is walking down the center aisle of the mall, and you hit the deck on the ground behind a candle display. Again, your cell phone should be turned to silent and you should remain quiet behind that display. Hopefully, if there is an active shooter, he doesn't spot you and come toward you. If you see people running and you maintain this defensive position, just like being barricaded in a retail store, it is very important that you and your family know how to act when the police come on the scene.

The first police that are going to respond to an active shooter situation are uniformed police who have

Hide and turn your phone on silent.

been trained to head in the direction of the shooter and try to neutralize the shooter or shooters as soon as possible. Their training techniques dictate how that has to be done. Years ago, the police would wait at the perimeter until the SWAT team would arrive, and by then the active shooter would normally have taken their own life after inflicting as much damage as they could. Now, the first officers you might see are ununiformed or they could be uniformed; every situation is different. Again, I would still maintain that position either in the store or hiding behind the candle display. After that, the SWAT team will be called in–they will come in and they will run through the store, usually in a diamond pattern, sweeping room-to-room. It's at this point when the police arrive and, whether you're hiding behind a barricaded door or lying on the floor behind some candles, you should follow these valuable tips. The first tip is to remain silent with your hands visible and wait for the police to give you direction. Do not talk, yell, or scream, because then you might give away the police's location to the active shooter if they're in hiding. Wait for the police to approach you. They will search you; they will treat you roughly, like a criminal. They don't know if you're the good guy or the bad guy. You must follow their commands. Normally, if they're clearing a mall or sports venue, the path is clear behind them and they will have people set up to send you to be searched, ID'd, and put in a holding area until they can sort the entire situation out. When a SWAT team arrives, this is a great time to give the police any valuable intel you may have witnessed: how many attackers there were, what they were wearing, what direction they were going in, etc.

These scenarios I've discussed are talking about you and your loved ones. There are so many other scenarios that need to be addressed if you're dealing with the elderly, the infirmed, or handicapped. What if you have four kids with you? What if you have your two kids and your neighbor's two kids? This could be a serious problem.

How are you going to keep them all quiet? Younger children will not realize the severity of the situation and will get fidgety, make noise, and say they're hungry, or "When are we leaving?," "When are we eating?," "I have to go to the bathroom," etc. This is why parents need to have a good grasp on their children and prepare them for every situation. Sometimes it's not always the best to be your child's friend. Sometimes it's better to be your child's parent.

When I go off into the world, I always carry a folding pocketknife, a small tactical flashlight, and an assortment of other goodies that I might not want to discuss. But imagine being trapped in an active shooter situation at a mall or sports venue, and you have these small tools at your disposal. A flashlight is especially important if the lights are shot out or purposely turned off. It's not a bad thing to have a couple of defensive tools. Visualize being in a mall, and the active shooter is coming through your barricade at the retail store, and you're able to momentarily blind him with a minimum of 120-lumen flashlight. That might just give you the upper hand. It's little training tips and tools like these that go a very long way.

As discussed previously, something to remember is that your cell phone should always be charged. I would hate to be hunkered down and barricaded in a retail store with only one battery bar left on my phone, a situation where I might be trapped for six, seven, eight, ten hours. Your phone is just like your car's gas tank. It should always be close to full. Who knows when something's going to happen? Always plan to prepare for the worst.

Go back to the Defensive Mindset and protect your most valuable assets, you and your family. Every opportunity you get to run through a training exercise with yourself and your loved ones in a public situation is one more lesson learned. These will be burned into your and your loved ones' brains should the shit hit the fan and you have to respond. It's very important to be aware of all of your surroundings. It is very important to know what a safe direction may or may not be, should you have to flee. It is very important to make sure you have the necessary belongings that you need, should you have to flee, because you may only have split seconds to react. As you're running, you'll be saying, "I should have, I could have, and I would have." It's very important to burn this into your loved ones' brains.

Something to consider is to maybe have an external rendezvous point. If you make it outside the mall in the parking lot by the entrance of Sears, the first thing you should text your loved ones is, "Put your phone on silent," just to remind them. Then tell them your position, and they should tell you their position. This might also help you to alert the authorities, and you'll have a little intel of what's going on inside the mall. Do not try to be a hero and go back into the mall to rescue your loved ones that you've been separated from. It will do no one any good if you're one of the people that becomes a victim. I know that emotions get involved, and it is very hard to refrain from something like that, but you have to look at the overall big picture and see what is better for you and your family."

Every school and campus should have a comprehensive plan for an active shooter situation today. For the most part, the plans should be strictly adhered to. I will just be offering a few more tips here for an added level of safety. If you are a parent, it is on you to make sure you are fully aware of the school's plans for an active shooter. You also have the right to question the policies. As discussed earlier in this chapter, the same rules apply with silencing your cell phone, finding cover or concealment, and how to respond when the police arrive. This is critical for everyone in the household to be aware of as well.

One of the biggest obstacles with training like this is trying to get your family and loved ones to understand the importance and severity. Since you're reading this book, you have this mindset. It's trying to get these people, the nay-sayers and the non-believers, to understand that this is real, and it could happen. It seems to be a little easier to get people on the same page as us these days. The frequency of active shooter situations and terrorist threats across the world have been increasing—well, the media coverage has for sure. The statistics behind all of this are complex and misleading, but nonetheless, people are starting to think, "Hey, maybe this could happen to me." Should you find yourself in such a tragic situation, keep calm and lean on what you have learned.

CHAPTER
19

Fitness and Disabilities

Let's face it, most Americans are not in the best of health, and many of us have a disability or two due to surgeries, etc. In order to defend yourself and your family, it is on you to be in the best physical shape you can be in in any circumstance. I was once 420 pounds and I could not lift myself up from a kneeling or prone position without using my arms to boost myself up! I could also not run up a flight of stairs without being winded. Imagine a stressful situation. Having a heart attack or not being able to physically defend yourself will not be helpful to you and yours during a crisis. If you

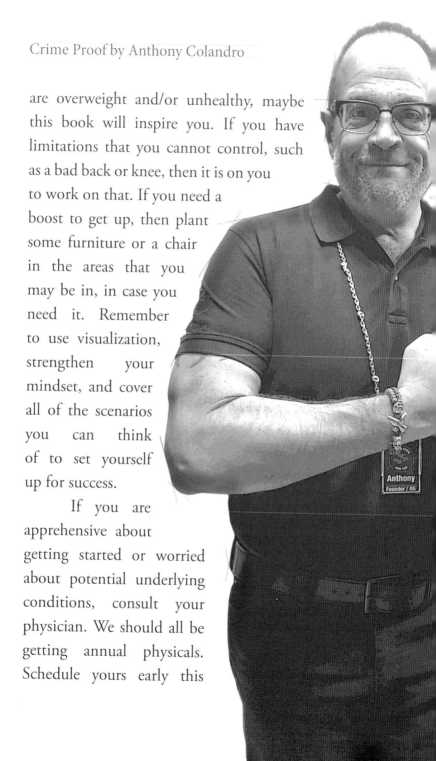

are overweight and/or unhealthy, maybe this book will inspire you. If you have limitations that you cannot control, such as a bad back or knee, then it is on you to work on that. If you need a boost to get up, then plant some furniture or a chair in the areas that you may be in, in case you need it. Remember to use visualization, strengthen your mindset, and cover all of the scenarios you can think of to set yourself up for success.

If you are apprehensive about getting started or worried about potential underlying conditions, consult your physician. We should all be getting annual physicals. Schedule yours early this

year and talk to your doctor about coming up with a health management plan.

If you have allowed the years to catch up to you and you've developed a stellar dad bod, start slow. Every journey, no matter how long, starts with the first step. Don't just jump into the gym and start lifting right where you left off ten, fifteen, or twenty years ago. If you do that, you may hurt yourself and/or become so sore that your desire to continue will dwindle quickly. So, come up with a plan that is right for you!

Americans have some of the worst diets in the world. If you can afford to shed some pounds, you are going to have to change your eating habits too. You created your masterpiece of a body in the kitchen, and you're going to have to fix it there too. No one likes the word "diet." You need to think lifestyle change. Just like getting more physically fit, you can start this slow. Take those protein bars that you have stashed away for a disaster, and replace a meal or two a week with them. Little things like that will add up. Sugary drinks and sodas should be completely cut out of your routine, even diet sodas. Exchange those for sparkling water if you need that extra kick in your drinks.

I'm not looking to be preachy here. You know what you have to do, and you can do it! All it takes is a little bit of dedication and willpower. It is never too late to start a journey to get in better shape. Personally, I box and train five days a week just so I can handle myself in a nasty situation. I have never felt better or more confident. I especially like kettlebells, and I practice holding them out in my hands hyperextended for as long as I can. I do this exercise ten sets at a time. All the while, I am visualizing holding a three-pound handgun on a bad guy until the police arrive in ten minutes or so. Not an easy task, try it!

Take it from a guy that woke up one day and said, "I gotta do something about this, or I'm going to die!" Even if you never have a violent situation or encounter in your life, which I hope you never do, you want to live long enough to be able to say so! Do this for yourself…do this for your family.

CHAPTER
20

Keeping Your Children Safe

Your children are your most valuable assets. It is our job, as parents, to safeguard them and cater to their needs. Beyond providing general sustenance and a place to live, it's a parent's role to raise a child that can stand on their own and will not be taken advantage of. There is a fine line between raising an aware child and one that will be afraid of their own shadow, so tread lightly. Throughout this book, the subject of children kept popping up, as did tips and tricks to keep them safe. Here are some general concepts and ideas to add to what we discussed outside of the context of a particular chapter.

One thing that you should teach your child is the concept of a secret password. What would this password be used for? For example, say little Johnny was at school and gets called to the main office. While at the office, Johnny's

uncle is there to pick him up. Johnny's uncle says that he was asked by his parent to pick him up and take him out of school early because of a family emergency. At this point, Johnny is supposed to ask his uncle the password. If his uncle does not have the password, Johnny is not supposed to go. Why? The majority of child kidnappings that happen involve people the child knows.

In today's world, many schools and daycares have lists of people that are allowed to come and pick up children. When you enroll your child into a daycare or when they start going to a particular school, find out about these polices. If they are not in place, the password technique is an added layer of protection. At school is not the only place that someone may be coming to abduct your child. What if Johnny's uncle comes to Johnny's friend's house when the two of them are having a playdate? This is a concept that you really need to think about.

When enrolling your child in a daycare, school, or other institution, ask the administrators about their security policies. Find out what their plans are in case of an emergency. A friend of mine was shopping around for daycares and found one that was promising. The daycare was located at a facility that used to be an elementary school and, in fact, there were two different daycares operating in the same building. They shared the space and there was nothing that physically separated the two businesses. While touring the building, my friend asked the administrator "Okay, I understand that there is another daycare here, right? So, if there is an emergency, who is ultimately in charge? Who is the main point of contact that will be handling all the kids if there is a fire? A shooting? Anything at all?" He said that the administrator stammered, made a flummoxed face, and then there was mostly silence. My friend looked at his wife and she just nodded. Needless to say, they did not enroll their child in that daycare. This is the kind of stuff you need to think about.

Children love personalized things. Anything that identifies them as an individual. Say your kid loves sharks, what do you end up with? Shark everything! Things that people get that are more harmful than helpful are articles of clothing or accessories with their child's name embroidered on them. All it takes is a stranger intent on harm to see your child's name, and then they have half the keys to the kingdom. With that information alone, they could easily sweet talk your kid away from wherever they are, and off to never be seen again.

Child sex trafficking and molestation are big problems today. You won't see it on the evening news all that often, but if you astutely watch the headlines in different news aggregates, you'll constantly find out about big child porn ring busts, large child trafficking operations uncovered, and all kinds of horrors. This is why it is so important to raise a child that is aware of today's dangers. An uncomfortable thing that you should consider discussing is your child's "private parts." We all have little pet names for our "no no" areas like "pee pee" and "biscuit." That is fine and dandy when you're having tub time, but teach your kid to be able to articulate what their anatomy is. Should the horrific event of molestation happen to your child, you want them to be able to clearly say "He touched my penis," or "He touched my vagina and put fingers in it." Sounds uncomfortable? That's because it is! In the aftermath of such an atrocity, you want no gray areas, you want it black and white…"This is EXACTLY what happened to me."

Other child safety concepts in this book should be reviewed often. Remember to teach your kid how to handle a stranger at the door. Take into consideration that tip involving using a dog tag when traveling with your child. Don't leave your kid in a shopping cart! Sign up with an organization that will help you put together a child abduction kit. Regularly have emergency drills in your home with them, teach them how to use a fire extinguisher, and how to dial 911. Raise your child to be aware of the sheep, wolves, and sheepdogs. Don't teach your kid that the police are bad and will lock them up if they do something they are not supposed to, but rather teach them that the police are who you go to if you need help—and live by that credo. Don't grumble about "some a-hole cop" when you're driving. Children are liabilities when it comes to the security of a family unit, but they are your liabilities, and you need to protect them with your life.

Conclusion

Okay, so you have read my book. Please do not put it on the shelf and forget about it. It is now your job to teach those that "don't think like this." The criminals are smart and always are getting smarter. They look for new ways to victimize us. So, please be vigilant, and stay safe.

Stand Strong!

Anthony P. Colandro
Capitalist Marksmen
Founder of Gun For Hire LLC

Resources

The National Rifle Association (NRA)
The NRA is America's premier Second Amendment Civil Rights organization. Originally formed to teach shooting skills to American Citizens, the NRA has many different programs and branches, all of which are worth exploring. If you are not a member of the NRA, consider joining. You can learn more about the NRA on their homepage: https://home.nra.org

State Firearm Associations
States have their own firearm associations affiliated with the NRA. These groups are your boots on the ground where you live. State associations are responsible for being a stopgap between your state government and the seizing of your civil rights. You can find out about any state associations where you live by visiting their homepage: https://stateassociations.nra.org

Association of New Jersey Rifle and Pistol Clubs (ANJRPC)
The Association of New Jersey Rifle and Pistol Clubs, Inc. is the official NRA State Association in New Jersey. Their mission is to implement all of the programs and activities at the state level that the NRA does at the national level. https://www.anjrpc.org

Decoding Firearms By John Petrolino

Decoding Firearms: An Easy to Read Guide on General Gun Safety and Use is a comprehensive book that covers all that a new gun owner, or one that wants to brush up, needs to know concerning the use of firearms. Decoding Firearms is available on Amazon as a paperback or in Kindle e-book format. For more information on *Decoding Firearms*, visit: https://johnpetrolino.com/decoding-firearms

National Shooting Sports Foundation (NSSF)

The NSSF is the firearms trade organization. They offer resources to both those engaged in commercial operations in the shooting world, as well as to ordinary citizens. NSSF has many programs for the public to take advantage of, such as suicide prevention and awareness programs, child firearm safety programs, and initiatives advocating for lawful firearm ownership. Learn more about the NSSF and the multitude of their projects on their homepage: https://www.nssf.org

Project Childsafe, one of NSSF's programs, is geared towards the responsible storage of firearms and has fantastic resources for gun owners. Learn about their initiatives and more on their homepage: https://projectchildsafe.org

US LawShield™

US LawShield is a membership program that offers different benefits to their members. They specialize in aiding their program members, should they need legal counsel in the event of lawful weapon use during self-defense. To learn more about their offerings and what their memberships include, visit them on their homepage: https://www.uslawshield.com

NY Tac Defense

NY Tac Defense is a New York based, prepaid legal service for gun owners. They offer 24/7 emergency response by defense attorneys, should you find yourself needing one. Read more about them on their homepage: https://nytacdefense.com

The Second Amendment Woman Shooting Club (SAW)

SAW shooting club is an organization created by women for women. Their focus is on offering guidance, education, and a social setting for women to come and exercise their Second Amendment rights. Learn more about SAW, what they do, and who they are on their homepage: http://sawshootingclub.com/

The 2nd is for Everyone

The 2nd is for Everyone Diversity Shoot is an organization that drops the barriers. The group's aim is to foster inclusiveness among those in or interested in the Second Amendment community regardless of race, color, creed, sex, sexual orientation, etc. Their main objective is to offer a space where anyone can come along to partake in the shooting sports. Learn more about The 2nd is for Everyone on their homepage:
http://www.diversityshoot.com/

The Coalition of New Jersey Firearm Owners (CNJFO)

CNJFO is a New Jersey-based not-for-profit outreach, education, and advocacy group. They believe that, by bringing people together in a social setting, great work can be done. CNJFO has hosted numerous educational events for women, children, and the public at large, as well as organized hunts and other social events. The Coalition has authored friend of the court briefs, notably one for the Cheeseman case, which was denied by the Supreme Court of The United States. To learn more about CNJFO, who they are, and what they do, visit them at their homepage: www.cnjfo.com

Attorney Evan Nappen

Licensed to practice law in New Hampshire and New Jersey, Evan Nappen is a veteran firearm attorney. With six books on firearms, a gun law podcast, numerous publications under his belt, and over 30 years of experience, Evan Nappen has seen what rotten laws can do to the law-abiding citizen. He's a fearsome courtroom litigator, fighting for rights, justice, and freedom. Nappen is the New Jersey affiliate attorney with USLawShield.
http://www.evannappen.com

Atienza Kali

From their website: Atienza Kali is a family system based on the skill and tactics of the Atienza family. The highest level of combat application is based on the movements of the family unit, four people, namely a father and his three sons, while engaging a mass of people. The Atienza Kali family system was developed to deal with a particular combat scenario—mass attack. It was common to see masses of people attacking others in the neighborhood they lived in during the 1980s. As a result of observing this, the Atienza family developed a system to deal with this problem.
https://atienzakali.com

The New Jersey Second Amendment Society (NJ2AS)

NJ2AS is a member organization that fights for the rights of New Jersey gun owners. NJ2AS has been involved in several victorious court battles with the State of New Jersey, and is a staunch advocate for the rights of law-abiding gun owners. To learn more about NJ2AS, you can find them online at their homepage:
www.nj2as.org

The Quarantine Crawl

The Quarantine Crawl, aka our "Chamber of Commerce," started as a video series that Anthony Colandro did during the COVID-19 lockdown in New Jersey. In order to help support second amendment friendly companies, Anthony would act as a surprise secret shopper, popping in to give patronage to mom-and-pop operations. A full catalog of Anthony's reviews and visits are available for viewing online. The Quarantine Crawl morphed into something bigger, especially as the COVID restrictions waned... Now, Colandro has a complete directory of Second Amendment friendly businesses so that you, the freedom lover, can support those who support you! Check out the comprehensive listing as well as the videos at:
https://quarantinecrawl.com

Knife Rights

From their mission statement, Knife Rights is dedicated to: Providing knife and edged tool owners an effective voice to influence public policy and to oppose efforts to restrict the right to own, use, and carry knives and edged tools; encouraging safe, responsible, and lawful use of knives and edged tools through education and outreach, enhancing positive perceptions of knives and edged tools and their owners and users; encouraging the marketing of knives and edged tools in a responsible manner conducive to the organization's goals; cooperating with advocacy organizations having complementary interests and goals; providing knife and edged tool owners with services that they will find valuable in order to build membership to enable success in our primary objectives.
https://kniferights.org

New Jersey Concealment Furniture

From their website: A family-owned business, N.J. Concealment Furniture acknowledges the fact that some of your personal items must be kept in a safer place. Their furniture store in Hampton, New Jersey, offers handmade furniture that you can use when you need extra protection for your possessions. All of their products are handcrafted using hardwood of the finest quality. They make stunning furniture that serves an even greater purpose. The furniture is exceptionally sturdy, including mortise and tenon, biscuit, dadoes, and miter lock joints. Carefully designed and crafted, the furniture can be passed down for generations to come.

https://njconceal.co

About The Author

Anthony P. Colandro is the owner of Gun For Hire Woodland Park Range and the host of the hit podcast show "Gun For Hire Radio," which has over one million listeners nationwide. He is a fervent believer in, and staunch advocate for, the "Right to Carry." He is the Executive Vice President of ANJRPC and has helped to defeat New Jersey legislative attacks against the rights of American citizens during 2013 and beyond.

Born in Newark, NJ in 1961 and raised in Belleville, NJ, Anthony graduated from Belleville High School in 1979. His loving and supportive family include his parents, Anthony Sr. and Florence Colandro, who currently reside in Woodland Park, NJ, and his brother Peter. Anthony has continued his lifelong pursuit of knowledge, personal experience, and peak performance. He now resides in Woodland Park, NJ.

After many successful years in the promotional advertising industry, Anthony decided to turn his passion into his livelihood. When Anthony founded Gun For Hire in 1992, his goals were to teach the positive aspects of self-awareness and defense and to promote the responsibilities of safe firearm ownership.

Along his professional journey, Anthony became an NRA Master Training Counselor. Only a select few enjoy this great honor in this very small fraternity from the USA! Colandro is also a student of Massad Ayoob, and graduated from his Lethal Force Institute in Concord, NH. Anthony continued to nurture and educate firearms enthusiasts and newcomers alike. Anthony operated Gun For Hire out of up to seven ranges during those early days, all in the tri-state area, while simultaneously cultivating and refining his own business.

Anthony was a trendsetter early in the industry by welcoming ALL into the firearm community. He donates to the SAW Group (Second Amendment Women) use of the range, classroom, instructors, and range officers, enabling them to host their events at his facility. The Woodland Park Range also was the first range to host Tony Simon's The Second is for Everyone Diversity shoots.

Gun For Hire Woodland Park Range opened in 2013, and is located in Woodland Park, NJ. It is the first and only family gun range destination in the world! Tens of thousands of law-abiding citizens every year are trained at The Woodland Park Range. The business has grown exponentially since 2013 and required a major extension, which tripled the size of the facility, in order to accommodate the demand for firearms training and safety courses.

The Woodland Park Range is one of the largest commercial ranges here in the United States now that the addition is complete. The range hosts more than 100 police departments to facilitate training and qualifications for law enforcement professionals. Additionally, Gun For Hire exclusively offers a high-level training division and security operation in order to support often overlooked aspects of police and security training.

Anthony is a major contributor to law enforcement causes and civilian benefit foundations throughout New Jersey. All new firearms and duty rigs for the entire Woodland Park Police department were procured by Anthony, and he hosts and supports countless other philanthropic ventures throughout the area. He is also known as the guy who never says "no!"

A passionate, aggressive, and outspoken defender of the Second Amendment, he has been a vigilant civil rights advocate for over 30 years in the battleground state of New Jersey. Anthony has been invited to speak for various TV and radio programs, notably Fox News, The Kelly File, and The Story with Martha Macallum. Anthony has been featured in numerous articles online and in print, to note: The Wall Street Journal, Medium, Vice, and many others. He can often be observed in the State House speaking his mind when he feels that the people need a bellicose liaison. He will "Stand Strong" against the throes of adversity to the endowments by our creator of "certain unalienable Rights…"

Anthony is also a National Rifle Association Board Member and sits on three committees, namely Education and Training, Clubs and Associations, and Range Development. He supports NRA competitive activities, including Women on Target®, Eddie Eagle®, and the NRA Civil Rights Defense Fund. Anthony has been an NRA Certified Instructor for over 30 years. He received the NRA Second Amendment Activist of the Year Award and the NRA Trainer of Distinction Award in 2018.

Anthony enjoys contributing his time, attention, and prosperity to numerous professional and civic organizations, and he is very active in supporting humanitarian causes to which he is deeply committed.